GERMAN
ARMORED WARFARE
OF WORLD WAR II

GERMAN
ARMORED WARFARE
OF WORLD WAR II
THE UNPUBLISHED PHOTOGRAPHS **1939–1945**

IAN BAXTER

CASEMATE
HAVERTOWN, PA

This edition first published in 2003 by

CASEMATE

2114 Darby Road
Havertown, PA 19083

Copyright © 2003 Amber Books Ltd

Library of Congress Cataloging-in-Publication Data available.

ISBN: 1-932033-15-7

Editorial and design by
Amber Books Ltd
Bradley's Close
74-77 White Lion Street
London N1 9PF

Project Editor: Mariano Kälfors
Editor: Caroline Curtis
Design: Graham Curd
Picture Research: Lisa Wren

Printed in Italy

Picture credits

Martin Kaludow: 32 (t), 52, 53 (t), 55, 59, 67, 76, 83 (b), 84 (b), 88 (t), 89 (b), P94, 101 (t), 111 (t), 111 (b), 123 (b), 127 (b), 161 (t), 170, 171 (t), 194(t), 194 (b), 195 (t), 217 (t).

Robert Michulec: 7, 22 (t & b), 34 (b), 35 (b), 36, 42 (t), 43 (both), 45 (t), 50 (b), 51 (t), 186 (both), 187 (both, 188 (both), 189 (b), 207 (t).

Sergey Zborski: 21 (b), 31 (t), 37 (b), 56 (b), 57, 91 (both), 101 (b), 167 (t).

**All other photographs are credited to HITM Picture Archive
www.militaria-net.co.uk/hitm.htm**

Contents

CHAPTER ONE

The Panzer Division

German Armour of World War II

In October 1935 the *Panzerwaffe* created the first three Panzer divisions. Initially a Panzer division comprised of two tank regiments. These regiments were divided into two battalions; each battalion was made up of four companies with 32 light tanks. The entire division strength amounted to some 561 Panzers, including command tanks. By 1940 a typical Panzer division comprised the Panzer divisional staff; two tank regiments; three rifle regiment detachments consisting mainly of halftracks and cross-country armoured cars; Panzer signals; Panzer engineers; reconnaissance; artillery regiment; motorcycle battalion; flak detachment; and supply vehicles that were primarily made up of trucks and transport vehicles. The whole division was made up of captured Czech Pz.Kpfw.35(t)s and Pz.Kpfw.38(t)s, Pz.Kpfw.Is, Pz.Kpfw.IIs, Pz.Kpfw.IIIs and Pz.Kpfw.IVs, a multitude of various armoured cars, heavy guns, haulage trailers and tractors. Both reconnaissance and engineers provided bridging, and printing and meteorological office troops were attached to the artillery regiment.

LEFT: A variety of vehicles, including various tanks, halftracks, Horch cross-country cars, and other supporting vehicles, spread out across the vast Russian steppe as a precaution against Soviet aerial attack. The number of vehicles that can be seen have all been painted with summer camouflage schemes, usually green and brown lines and patches applied over a dark sand base. By the time winter arrives, the vehicles will have received a new camouflage application of whitewash.

LEFT: An assault gun battery is on its way to the frontline of the Eastern Front in July 1941. In the heat of the midday sun, a column of StuG.IIIs moves along one of the many dirt roads that crossed the Soviet countryside. The situation and terrain of the area, especially in Russia, sometimes made it necessary to have the supply staff located alongside the assault gun battery. Their vehicles stayed to the rear when the assault guns advanced or penetrated the enemy defences. In the Russian campaign the assault guns were detailed to the infantry divisions that fought at local points in the battles.

With these new Panzer divisions the German Army sought not to attempt to outflank the enemy and envelop him, but to destroy his forces on the field of battle, using the weight and speed of the Panzer divisions to break through the enemy line and head for vital objectives deep within the enemy rear. The decisive weapon in this new style of warfare was, without a doubt, the massed tanks of the Panzer divisions. While the Panzers raced forward towards their strategic objectives, the rest of the division's units followed through the gap that they had created. Armoured cars, motorcycles and reconnaissance units then moved forward, while the motor rifle battalions were following closely behind the Panzers, ready at all time to deal with the least sign of resistance along the divisional sector. Motorized artillery followed, ready to give any fire support to the advancing armour or infantry units. Anti-tank guns provided protection against enemy tank counter-attack.

On mobilization in August 1939 the five Panzer divisions poised to invade Poland in September were still under-gunned and under-armoured, possessing only enough Panzers to equip three of their four tank companies. The Panzer divisions did have the edge over the antiquated Polish armoured units, but only with fire-control equipment and inter-tank radio communications were they clearly superior. The main German advantage during the invasion of Poland, as later in the West in 1940 and on the Eastern Front in 1941, lay not in what equipment the Panzer divisions possessed, but how they were utilized on the battlefield.

In Poland the five Panzer divisions were deployed against a brave but badly equipped, out-of-date Polish army. Their cavalry and mechanized units were clearly no match against even the lightest of Panzers. Still, out of the 2100 Panzers fielded against the Poles, 213 were lost during the three-week campaign, with 57 of them in one single day, attempting to storm Warsaw. More serious than the loss of Panzers in battle though was the high rate of mechanical failure, which kept 25 per cent of the machines out of action at any one time. Nor was there any improvement by the time the *Panzerwaffe* unleashed ten Panzer divisions against the West in 1940. Out of the 2574 Panzers, fewer than 627 were of the heaviest Pz.Kpfw.III and Pz.Kpfw.IV types, and 1613 were the obsolete Pz.Kpfw.I and II. Nonetheless, in just five weeks the Panzer divisions, with the rest of the Army trailing behind, had roared through France to the Channel coast and a German victory was beckoning.

The Panzers had shown their worth and mastered not only the local terrain, but Allied tanks as well. Both the British and French tank crews fought courageously, but the outcome was almost always settled by the superiority of Panzer skills and techniques. By the time a German victory was sealed with an armistice signed on 22 June 1940, the *Panzertruppen* and their mighty Panzer divisions had become heroes among the men of the German Army. They had netted more than 250,000 prisoners in a Blitzkrieg of just 13 days and had established the importance of using armour in the forefront of battle. As a result, it became clear that the *Panzerwaffe* should now be considered the equal of the infantry. With the West now defeated, Hitler became more eager than ever to expand the *Panzerwaffe* and demanded tank production be increased five-fold.

Just weeks later, inspired by the triumph against the Allies, Hitler began hastily drawing up plans for a campaign against Russia. Guderian was dismayed, but Hitler assured him that he aimed to double the number of Panzer divisions for the coming battle. He was soon to raise the number of Panzer divisions from 10 to 21 by halving the AFV (Armoured Fighting Vehicle) strength of each division. Thus, the core of each new Panzer division consisted of a single tank regiment numbering some 150–200 machines: Hitler, intoxicated by success in the West, was now convinced that a Panzer division fielding a single armoured regiment was a strong as two regiments. This was a fatal error on Hitler's part, especially since the armaments factories were not equipped for mass production of AFVs. During the first half of 1941, they

BELOW: A number Pz.Kpfw.IIIs Ausf.F line up on the Eastern Front in 1941. During this early period of the campaign, most of the tanks were still painted in their old grey camouflage scheme. Some of the tank crews have applied foliage to the front of the tanks in order to break up the shape of the vehicle.

The tanks still retain the early style of tactical numbering – white painted numbers on a black, rhomboid metal plate. These tanks mounted a 3.7cm (1.46in) KwK L/46.5 gun and saw action extensively in until 1942, when they were withdrawn from frontline service and used as training vehicles for new recruits.

ABOVE: A group of Pz.Kpfw.Is in action on the Western Front in May 1940 move across a field. Pz.Kpfw.Is were still in service up the time of the German assault on the Low Countries and France. The vehicles are advancing in close formation, indicating that air domination has been achieved. During the invasion of the Low Countries and France, the Panzer divisions used strength and momentum to break through the enemy line and head for vital objectives deep within enemy territory.

were having serious difficulty producing more than 200 vehicles each month. By early June 1941, the total number of Panzers produced for the new war against Russia was 5262, of which 4198 were frontline Panzers, and of that total, only 1404 were up-gunned and strengthened Pz.Kpfw.IIIs and IVs. It seemed quantity was now to take precedence over quality; the seeds of disaster for the Panzer divisions were already being sown.

In the third week of June 1941, the *Panzerwaffe* managed to field some 3000 Panzers for the army assembled to invade the Soviet Union. These vehicles were distributed among 19 Panzer divisions, 10 motorized infantry divisions, 4 motorized SS divisions, the motorized *Grossdeutschland* Regiment and a few independent assault-gun units. Without doubt, the mobility and striking power of the Panzer divisions and other independent formations had convinced those in command that Germany would be victorious within four months of attacking Russia. However, the vast expanses of terrain that the vehicles had to cover, and the huge logistical problems, gave the army serious difficulties, particularly when the weather changed and the Soviets put up a stubborn defence.

In theory, the advantages lay entirely with the powerful Panzer divisions. Indeed, the *Panzerwaffe* had initially made spectacular progress, encircling almost half a million Russian soldiers within one month, but the Panzer and motorized divisions still had the limitless expanse of the Soviet Union ahead of them – thousands of miles. As the Panzers penetrated deeper and deeper into Russia, the road surfaces became much worse, and a heavy downfall of rain quickly changed the dirt roads into a quagmire where armoured vehicles became bogged down.

By October and November 1941, the Panzer divisions were still fighting deep inside Russia. Confronted by bitter opposition, they soon also had to deal with a harsh Russian winter that none of the soldiers were prepared for. Many units were worn down to half strength, and the Panzers were down to two-fifths of their original tank strength. Food was short, ammunition and fuel for the Panzers were running out, and still no winter clothing had arrived. By the end of 1941, the battle-weary Panzer divisions were no longer fit to fight. Fortunately, no mobile operations were envisaged for the winter. Instead, while the front lines remained immobilized in the snow, most of the Panzer divisions were pulled out and transferred to France, in order to rest, reorganize and re-train.

In Germany more Panzer divisions were frantically being raised, and motorized divisions being converted into Panzergrenadier divisions. For 1942, a further three Panzer divisions, Nos. 22, 23 and 24 were raised. However, equipping the new Panzer divisions was a very slow process due to the massive losses on the Eastern Front. By the beginning of the summer offensive in May 1942, not all were yet fully equipped for action. All three newly created Panzer divisions were deployed in the south, with the best-equipped Panzer divisions being concentrated in Army Group South for the attack in the Caucasus. The new divisions had a combined strength of 495 Panzers, 181 of which were concentrated in the 24th Panzer Division.

In September 1942 a further two Panzer divisions were formed to help bolster the strength on the Eastern Front. However, by January 1943, the 14th, 16th, and 24th Panzer divisions had been lost at Stalingrad. The end in Russia seemed inevitable, but Hitler was determined to pour as many resources as possible into the badly depleted armoured force. Then came another terrible blow for the Panzer units: in May 1943 in Tunisia the 10th, 15th and 21st Panzer divisions were lost with the surrender of the German forces in North Africa. Only the 21st Panzer division would be reformed.

Throughout the spring of 1943, the *Panzerwaffe* had been building up its strength and by the summer fielded some 24 Panzer divisions on the Eastern Front. Four Panzer divisions were also deployed in Italy and Sicily; five Panzer divisions, including three new SS Panzer divisions, were stationed in France; and one, the 1st Panzer division, was in the Balkans. By June 1943, 21 Panzer divisions, including four SS and two Wehrmacht Panzergrenadier divisions were prepared for Operation Citadel on the Eastern Front. For this massive tank battle – the largest of World War II – the *Panzerwaffe* were able to put together some 17 divisions and 2 brigades with no less than 1715 Panzers and 147 StuG.III assault guns. Each division

averaged some 98 Panzers and self-propelled guns, not including self-propelled anti-tank guns. It was a great achievement to muster such a force, but the Panzer division of 1943 was a mere shadow of the strength it had during the battles of 1941 and 1942. It was therefore not surprising that the armoured force was unable to break through the strong Russian defensive positions. The losses the Panzer division sustained at Kursk were so immense that the German Army took the first steps of its slow retreat back to Germany. The Soviets had managed to destroy 30 divisions, seven of which were Panzer. German reinforcements were insufficient to replace the staggering losses, so they fought on under-strength.

During the last half of 1943 and early 1944, losses to the Panzer divisions continued to escalate. So bad did losses become that they were greater than those sustained at Kursk. Both on the Eastern Front and the Italian Front, the Panzer divisions withdrew. By June 1944, when Overlord opened up the Allied second front in Europe, the *Panzerwaffe* had lost some 7500 Panzers and self-propelled guns in twelve months. Despite these losses, there were nine Panzer divisions stationed in France with 1673 Panzers and assault guns. On the Eastern Front there were 16 Panzer divisions with 1390 Panzers and two

BELOW: Late May 1940, northern France – and again the 7th Panzer Division is on the move. Spread out across the landscape, a multitude of vehicles push towards the Channel coast. Opel *Blitz* trucks and Horch cross-country cars follow

behind the main spearheads some miles ahead. The heavy Horch cross-country cars feature MG 34 machine guns; note the lightweight Dreifuss 34 antiaircraft mount and a 50-round Gurttrommel 34 'basket' magazine and ring sight.

ABOVE: Pz.Kpfw.38(t)s advance through northern France during the French campaign. These tanks, of Czechoslovakian design, were the principal armour used by the Germans in the early years of the war. Armed with a main 3.7cm (1.46in) cannon and two Czech type 37 (MG 37) 7.92mm (0.31in) machine-guns (one co-axial, one hull-mounted), the vehicle outflanked the slow-moving French tanks and easily penetrated their weaker side armour and tracks. The large tactical numbers on the side of the turrets are painted in red with a white outline. The tank with the tactical number 'I02' is a command vehicle.

Panzer divisions in Italy with some 350. However, within two months of the Allied landings in Normandy, the British and American forces had virtually destroyed the Panzer divisions concentrated in the West. Most of the heavy Panzers such as the Tigers and Panthers were lost, including the majority of Flakpanzers and their heavy trucks, guns and equipment. Even after the failed Ardennes offensive in December 1944, most of the Panzer divisions continued to fight on until the last days of the war. The Panzer divisions had by then become so badly depleted that the divisions were organized into ad hoc groups. With insufficient fuel or incorrect ammunition supplies, desperation filled the ranks.

When the end for the *Panzerwaffe* finally came in early May 1945, it had 2023 Panzers, 738 assault guns and 159 Flakpanzers left. The numbers were almost similar to that which had attacked Russia in 1941, but the situation four years later was very different. Undermined by severe lack of provisions it was unable to withstand the two-pronged Allied attack. The Panzer division survived the war, but not as the offensive weapon that had seen it win the early campaigns of 1939 and 1940.

RIGHT: A German propaganda postcard printed after the victorious French campaign shows an aerial view of a column of Pz.Kpfw.38(t)s driving towards the front. Behind the column on another road is a line of halftracks and Horch cross-country cars, together with motorcycle combinations. By the summer of 1940, the *Panzertruppen*, and its mighty Panzer divisions, had become heroes among the men of the German Army. Moreover, its success meant that the *Panzerwaffe* would soon rise to become the infantry's equal partner.

ABOVE: Another propaganda postcard, which was distributed throughout Germany following the victorious conclusion of the Western campaign. This aerial view shows armoured vehicles pouring across an intact bridge, probably in Belgium. The British and French tank crews fought courageously but to no avail. Three days afer the initial attack against the Low Countries, the Panzers had reached the Meuse River, sweeping back the bewildered British and French forces.

RIGHT: The latter stages of the French campaign. A German crossing point has been established and soldiers of an unidentified Panzer division are moving men and equipment across a river on pontoon rafts. The necessity of moving such critical heavy equipment, especially weighty armour, meant that the troops had little choice but to manhandle it laboriously across the river. The soldiers on the near bank of the river belong to the *Gebirgsjäger* (mountain troops).

ABOVE: A pontoon bridge has been erected across a river in Belgium, allowing light and medium Horch cross-country vehicles and Opel *Blitz* trucks to continue their advance in the wake of the armoured spearheads. Despite the huge shortages of vehicles in the Panzer divisions, there were no less than 100 different types of commercial lorries. The motorcyclist on his BMW R75 motorcycle is carefully directing his machine along the steel trusses of the bridge. These troops are part of the 1st *Gebirgs*-Division that fought as part of 1st Panzer Army in the Donetsk area in the spring of 1942.

BELOW: Early autumn 1941, western Russia – a convoy of light Horch cross-country vehicles, laden with soldiers, begins to move off on a dirt road. Two soldiers raising the coloured signal batons are probably members of a *Feldgendarmerie* unit.

The batons were used to direct traffic, signalling to the driver or other members of the *Feldgendarmerie*. In this instance, the drivers have been given the go-ahead to proceed forward. The road surface has been broken up by heavy traffic.

LEFT: Late May 1940, northern France – a column of Sd.Kfz.251 halftracks passes a StuG.III Ausf.A on a road. The tactical sign painted in white on the left mudguard indicates this vehicle is from the 1st Panzer Division. The letter 'G' on the right headlamp cover is the first letter of its commander, General Heinz Guderian. The 1st Panzer Division was the vanguard of the German advance through the Ardennes and met significant resistance during the early phases of the campaign in the West.

ABOVE: An unusual grave marks the resting place of three crewmembers of an Sd.Kfz.250 halftrack, killed during fierce fighting in Russia in mid-1943. It features a piece of the vehicle and three steel helmets. The first such military graves were Russian. It remained rare among soldiers of the German Army to build resting places for their war dead, though a number of units, especially those belonging to the *Panzerwaffe*, copied their enemy's methods as a mark of respect to the dead.

ABOVE: Under the shelter of some trees, Panzer crewmen have time to relax and enjoy a pot of tea (presumably from a looted teapot). One of the officers, from Rommel's 7th Panzer Division, is still wearing his black Panzer officer's *Feldmütze*. The officer-grade side cap was popular among the men who wore it, because of its smart appearance and comfort. Furthermore, inside an armoured vehicle it could be worn with the communications headphones without losing its distinctive shape. The insignia of the Panzer *Feldmütze* was made up of the national eagle and the cockade.

RIGHT: A Pz.Kpfw.III Ausf.G, armed with a powerful 5cm (1.97in) KwK L/42 gun, moves forward across the Russian steppe following intensive fighting inside an unknown town. The tank was also armed with two 7.92mm (0.312in) MG 34 machine-guns (one on the hull, one co-axial). It weighed 22.2 tonnes (21.8 tons) and carried a crew of five. The stowage bins can be clearly seen on the rear of the tank. In fact, as losses of transport vehicles mounted, the Germany Army was frequently forced to rely on armoured vehicles to move stores and equipment.

ABOVE: July 1943, Kursk – and Russian prisoners are led away. In the background, a number of armoured vehicles are spread out across the Steppe. The battle of Kursk was the swansong of the *Panzerwaffe*. In total, the Germans were able to put together 17 divisions and 2 brigades, having no less than 1715 tanks and 147 StuG.III assault guns. Each Panzer division averaged 98 tanks and self-propelled guns, not including self-propelled anti-tank guns.

ABOVE: On the Eastern Front, two Pz.Kpfw.IIIs have halted inside a village. This photograph was probably taken in Army Group Centre during the spring of 1942. By this point, the German Army had already lost its chance of victory, having based it mobility on wheels rather than tracks: Panzer forces with tracked transport might have overrun Russia's vital sectors long before the autumn rains, despite the bad roads. Up to the end of 1941, the *Panzerwaffe* had enjoyed complete tank superiority, but the following year the situation had been reversed. As a result, General Heinz Guderian was desperate to speed up the production of the Pz.Kpfw.III and Pz.Kpfw.IV, as well as beef up their existing armour.

ABOVE: In front of staff members General Erwin Rommel, also known as the 'Desert Fox', discusses the next movements of his Panzer force in the North African desert in 1942. Rommel was perhaps the greatest German military tactician of World War II, and here in North Africa, where he was to achieve his greatest successes, he gained the reputation of being unstoppable. He had already made a name for himelf in 1940, when his famous 7th Panzer Division steamrolled through France to victory.

RIGHT: In North Africa a crewmember relaxes on the engine deck of a Pz.Kpfw.III. Even at the best of times, tanks were very uncomfortable vehicles. Out in the desert the stifling heat made the experience of serving inside a tank almost unbearable. Many tank crews served dressed only in shorts and canvas shoes and spent lulls in the fighting out of their baking steel boxes. This particular tank has a makeshift aerial attached. The vehicle also serves as a washing line and has a canvas sheeting fastened to the side of the tank to provide the crew some shade from the blistering midday sun.

ABOVE: A Pz.Kpfw.III has halted somewhere in the western Sahara desert in 1942. A host of provisions are stowed on the rear of the engine deck. The Pz.Kpfw.III was used in North Africa as the main striking force in attack. Its powerful 5cm (1.97in) gun gave it advantage over other tanks that it encountered in the desert. The Panzer utilized the expansive desert terrain to great effect and frequently advanced in mass formation, with lines of tanks at intervals, advancing in waves. Panzer crews found that the relatively close formation was easier to control than a dispersed one.

ABOVE: A Pz.Kpfw.III armed with a 5cm (1.97in) gun moves along a dusty road in North Africa in 1942. Not only did the Pz.Kpfw.III prove its worth in the deserts of North Africa but was successful in other theatres of war as well. During the early years of the war the Pz.Kpfw.III was the main battle tank of the Panzer divisions and was the most common tank in North Africa in 1942. Around this time however, in response to growing encounters with superior allied tanks, the Germans began developing new tanks as well as upgunning existing models. This included modifying the Pz.Kpfw.III with a short-barrelled infantry suport gun that originally equipped the Pz.Kpfw.IV model.

RIGHT: A *Flakpanzer-kampfwagen IV* (2cm Flakvierling 38) Sd.Kfz.161/4 self-propelled anti-tank gun known as the *Wirbelwind*. These vehicles were constructed on a Pz.Kpfw.IV chassis with thick armoured plating welded to the front of the hull. By July 1944, 17 of them were completed and were issued to various units by September 1944. This particular *Wirbelwind* has been well camouflaged with lots of pieces of foliage attached to the main superstructure. By this period of the war the Allies had virtually destroyed all the Panzer divisions concentrated in the West. Between June and September 1944 it was reported that over 1,600 tanks, self-propelled guns and *Panzerjäger* had been totally destroyed on the Western Front alone.

BELOW: On the Eastern Front in late summer of 1941. The crew of a Pz.Kpfw.38(t) pose for the camera after the tank has been unloaded from its train transport. The 38(t) was used widely during the early part of the war and saw extensive action in Russia during the initial invasion. However it was severely undergunned hence a number of variants were introduced. These included flamethrower tanks, in which the hull machine gun was replaced by a flamethrower; additional armoured protection; and rearmament with the German-made 3.7cm (1.46in) KwK 35/36 L/46.5 gun. Increased demand for heavier armour and armament though soon relegated the Pz.Kpfw.38(t) to second-line duties such as reconnaissance and service in armoured trains by 1942.

RIGHT: Late summer 1941, on the road to Moscow. These vehicles – Horch cross-country cars, prime movers and a motorcycle combination – belong to General Heinz Guderian's *Panzergruppe II* of Army Group Centre. Guderian's *Panzergruppen* contained the largest number of German infantry and Panzer divisions of the three Army groups that attacked the Soviet Union in June 1941. Among the three Panzer corps, there were some 930 tanks. The letter 'G' painted in white on the right mudguard of a light Horch cross-country car indicates that it belongs to Guderian's *Panzergruppen.*

ABOVE: A StuG.III laden with Panzergrenadiers moves through the devastated city of Stalingrad during September 1942. Note the machine gunner armed with an MG 34 on the front of the assault gun. Although armoured vehicles were less successful when embroiled in urban combat than when operating on open terrain, the assault gun became an important weapon and their crews followed their own infantry or Panzer troops everywhere. During the early fighting at Stalingrad, the assault guns were able to provide the hard-hitting infantry with valuable support. The StuG's main task was primarily to support the infantry in attacks. With a low silhouette (to improve its chances of survival), plus a dual armour-piercing and high explosive capability, the assault gun provided the infantry with a potent weapon on the battlefield. Because the vehicle was designed as a close support weapon, it carried a number of high-explosive, smoke and armour-piercing rounds.

ABOVE: A Panzer crewmember belonging to the *Waffen-SS* is congratulated after receiving the Knights Cross for his bravery in the field. He is wearing the SS-Panzer M43 *Feldmütze* with skull and cross bone insignia, and the standard reed green, two-piece protective clothing that was issued to all armoured *Waffen-SS* crews prior to January 1944.

RIGHT: As with all tanks the effectiveness of its main gun depended on the penetration ability of the armour piercing rounds. It was therefore imperative that the crews were equipped with shells that could deal with any threat. In this photograph the crew of a Tiger I are carefully loading the shells through the hatch. Of the total load of 92 rounds, half were armour-piercing, capped, ballistic capped with explosive filler and tracer, while the remainder were ordinary high-explosive shells. When available, high velocity, sub-calibre, tungsten core shells were used by crews, primarily against the heaviest armoured Russian tanks and tank destroyers.

RIGHT: Soldiers and vehicles from General Guderian's 1st Panzer Division in the Ardennes. While engineers prepare to erect a pontoon bridge across the river, members of a flak gun unit can be seen on a platform with their 2cm (0.79in) Flak light anti-aircraft gun. In the background, an Sd.Kfz.251 has just forded the river. Behind the halftrack, two Opel *Blitz* trucks have decided to brave the water in a drastic attempt to reach the other side.

BELOW: On the road to Dunkirk, a German officer has dismounted from the BMW motorcycle combination in which he was a passenger and is presumably waiting for his driver. He is wearing the practical, double-breasted, rubberized motorcycle coat that was issued to all soldiers, regardless of rank. He is also wearing an Army officer's *Schirmmütze* cap. By 1940 a typical Panzer division included a large motorcycle battalion, which was given various roles, including reconnaissance and communications duties, and was also used in combat, the soldiers riding into battle and dismounting to fight. On soft ground or on bad roads, the motorcycle was rendered largely useless. Riders were also vulnerable to small-arms fire and booby-traps. However, both in Poland and in the first French campaign, the weather was exceptionally good and motorcyclists were untroubled by the terrors of rain, mud and snow, which could turn a normal road system into a quagmire within a matter of minutes.

CHAPTER TWO

Main Battle Tanks

The Might of the *Panzerwaffe*

The Pz.Kpfw.III, IV, Panther and Tiger tanks were the backbone of the *Panzerwaffe*, combining a formidable mix of firepower, armour and mobility that outclassed most of their opponents.

Pz.Kpfw.III

In 1936 Daimler-Benz produced the first model of the Pz.Kpfw.III Ausf.E with an armour piercing weapon. The plan was for this Panzer type to equip three light companies of tank battalions. The tank was powered by a Maybach DSO twelve-cylinder high-performance 108 TR 11 litre petrol engine, giving a top speed of 40km/h (25mph). It was the *Panzerwaffe*'s first medium Panzer and was the first of six variants produced before July 1940; later versions were fitted with the more powerful 120 TR engine. Models A to F mounted a 3.7cm (1.46in) KwK L/46.5 gun and saw action extensively in all theatres of war until 1942, when they were finally withdrawn from frontline service and used as training vehicles for new recruits.

In April 1940, the Pz.Kpfw.III Ausf.G entered service and was armed with a more powerful 5cm KwK L/42 gun. Some 450 vehicles were produced up to February 1941, while German factories produced a further 310 Pz.Kpfw Ausf.H that received additional all-round armoured plating. The subsequent variant was the Pz.Kpfw.III Ausf.J. A few hundred of them featured bolted 5cm (2in) frontal armour, while subsequent Ausf.J models mounted a very powerful long-barrelled 5cm (1.97in) KwK 39 L/60 gun. In total there were some 2516 Ausf.J models built between March 1941 and July 1942.

Between June and December 1942, the Pz.Kpfw.III Ausf.L came off the production line and featured the same potent KwK 39 L/60 gun as the Ausf.J. Late that same year the Ausf.M entered service and incorporated a number of small modifications to its chassis, including the introduction of *schürzen*, an armoured side skirts intended primarily to protect the wheels and tracks from hollow-charge anti-tank weapons. Some 292 Ausf.M types were built between October 1942 and February 1943. By this time the *Panzerwaffe* had already recognized the growing inferiority of the Pz.Kpfw.III on the battlefield, but the armaments factories continued constructing these machines to offset the massive losses sustained on the Eastern Front. The last Pz.Kpfw.III model to be produced was the Ausf.N. This vehicle was primarily designed for heavy close fire-support, and was soon nicknamed the Sturmpanzer III. It was armed with a short-barrelled 7.5cm (2.95in) KwK L/24 gun that was previously mounted on a Pz.Kpfw.IV. More than 666 Ausf.N types were built between late 1942 and late 1943.

In August 1943, after some 5600 Pz.Kpfw.IIIs had been built, production finally halted in favour of the larger more powerful Pz.Kpfw.IV and the StuG III assault gun. Before its demise the Pz.Kpfw.III had undoubtedly shown its

LEFT: General Heinz Guderian on the Eastern Front in 1941. One of the most brilliant Panzer generals of World War II, Guderian was the man who formulated the concept of *Blitzkrieg* and transformed an outdated German Army into the greatest fighting machine of its time.

FAR LEFT: August 1942, southern Russia – this group of Pz.Kpfw.IIIs belongs to the 16th Panzer Division, as indicated by the divisional tactical sign painted in white on the left side of the driver's letterbox hatch.

ABOVE: 1940, and during the invasion of France two Pz.Kpfw.IV Ausf.D are attempting to bulldoze through a wall. The Pz.Kpfw.IV became the most popular Panzer of World War II and remained in production throughout the war. The tank weighed 17.3 tonnes (17 tons) and early variants mounted a powerful short-barrelled 7.5cm (2.95in) KwK L/42 gun.

worth on the battlefield: the machine contributed to the glorious successes of the German *Blitzkrieg* in 1940 on the Western Front and also during the first few weeks of the opening phases of Operation Barbarossa. However, against formidable Russian armour such as the T-34 medium and KV-1 heavy tanks, the Pz.Kpfw.III was soon recognized as an inadequate weapon. Panzer crews were frequently horrified at seeing rounds fired by its 5cm (1.97in) KwK L/42 gun fail to penetrate the frontal armour of the KV-1, even at short ranges; and the sloping plates of the T-34 rendered them virtually immune to fire. It was therefore not surprising that when these Panzer types fought in Kursk in July 1943, most were decimated in the tank battle. This battle proved to be the last great armoured encounter in which the Pz.Kpfw.III was involved in large numbers.

A year later the Pz.Kpfw.III had been largely relegated from the Panzer divisions to training units. Only a handful were ever seen in combat again, with a number of them deployed for action against Russian armour in northern Russia, in the Baltic states and in northern Italy during early 1945.

Pz.Kpfw.IV

The Pz.Kpfw.IV became the most popular Panzer of World War Two and remained in production throughout the war. At first it was not intended to be the main armoured vehicle in the *Panzerwaffe*, but it soon proved to be so diverse and effective that it became the most widely used of all the main battle tanks during the conflict. The first Pz.Kpfw.IV left the production line in 1936. The Ausf.A weighed 17.3 tonnes (17 tons) and mounted a powerful short-barrelled 7.5cm (2.95in) KwK L/24 gun. Its unique superstructure allowed the Panzer to be up-gunned later in the war. In 1939 a new variant Pz.Kpfw.IV Ausf.D was introduced, featuring heavier armour. Following the Polish and Western Front campaigns, where it saw its debut, Hitler ordered increased production of the Pz.Kpfw.IV. Subsequently a number of Ausf.E entered service between December 1940 and March 1941. During this period, tank planners were already designing another Pz.Kpfw.IV variant, the Ausf.F1. The production of this Panzer was in immediate response to the heavier Allied tanks confronted during the Western Front campaign in 1940. Between February 1941 and March 1942, some 975 Ausf.F1 Panzers were delivered to the front lines and some 548 of them were ready for action at the start of the invasion of Russia.

In March 1942 the production of the Pz.Kpfw.IV Ausf.F2 began. The vehicle was up-gunned with a long-barrelled 7.5cm (2.95in) KwK 40 L/43 gun and proved to be more than capable of knocking out the Soviet T-34. During the summer of 1942, yet another variant entered service on the Eastern Front, the Pz.Kpfw.IV Ausf.G, with enhanced armoured protection and an improved muzzle brake on the main 7.5cm (295in) gun. In total, some 1724 Pz.Kpfw.IV Ausf.F and G tanks saw action on the battlefields of Russia. A number of Ausf.G machines even included a longer 7.5cm (2.95in) L/48 gun from late 1942.

The following year, in early 1943, the Pz.Kpfw.IV Ausf. H entered service. With improved all-round armoured plating, it had an increased weight of 25 tonnes (24.6 tons) and a reduced top speed of 38kph (21mph). In total there were some 4000 Ausf.H types that saw action from the spring of 1943 onwards and this variant dominated the Panzer divisions in which it served. The last variant to be produced was the Ausf.J, which entered service in March 1944. With modified suspension and larger fuel tanks, 2392 of these Panzers spearheaded the elite tank battalions during the last year of the war.

Between 1936 and 1945 a total of 8472 Pz.Kpfw.IV were produced. For the better part of the war the Pz.Kpfw.IV was a match for its opponents. The tank had quickly demonstrated its superiority on the battlefield early on, so much so that it spearheaded the German Citadel offensive at Kursk in 1943. The offensive was a decisive failure but, despite sustaining great losses, the Pz.Kpfw.IV played a prominent role in the desperate attempt to halt the Soviet onslaught. On the battlefields of the Western Front too, despite inferior numbers, the tank performed well in defensive operations, and achieved resounding success with the elite *Waffen-SS* divisions. In December 1944, the Ausf.J spearheaded the Ardennes offensive but, by this period, not even the latest Pz.Kpfw.IVs or the other specialized variants, like the Flakpanzers, could counter the latest Allied tanks and hold the Allied advance at bay.

PANTHER

The Panther tank was a potent fighting weapon and was by far the best German tank of the Second World War. Planners primarily designed the Panther for action on the Eastern Front, with the intent of outclassing and achieving superiority over the T-34, and thereby halt the momentum of the Soviet offensive.

In January 1942 a 30-tonne (29.5-ton) prototype medium Panther came off the production line for the first time. With sloped armour, a powerful 650bhp Maybach HL 210 engine, interleaved wheels with torsion bar suspension, and a hydraulically powered turret with a new potent long-barrelled 7.5cm (2.95in) KwK L/70 gun, this beast was sped into mass production upon Hitler's orders. In November 1942, production commenced at an aggressive rate with the introduction of the Panther Ausf.D. It featured a larger engine and a more reliable and sturdy gearbox. Operated by a five-man crew, the Panther Ausf.D possessed very thick frontal and side armoured plating. To increase its armoured protection, factories welded on *schürzen* that were 5mm (0.2in) thick.

Despite numerous mechanical problems during trials, Hitler was adamant to rush the Panther into service as he regarded the tank critical to the future of the war effort. With Operation Citadel pending, Hitler ignored the obvious weaknesses of the Panther and ordered the High Command to produce two Army Panzer battalions containing Panthers to spearhead the Kursk offensive. Some 250 Panther Ausf.D tanks were allocated to the attack. When Citadel was finally unleashed on 4 July 1943, the Panther got off to a bad start, losing 125 on the first day. By the end of the second day, only 50 out of the original 250 were still operational. A number of the Panthers developed mechanical faults, and on others badly ventilated engines caught fire.

Following the disaster at Kursk, it was considered that the Panther Ausf.D was unsuitable for frontline operations and production was consequently halted. However, a late-production Ausf.D was produced soon afterwards. The

RIGHT: A Pz.Kpfw.IV Ausf.D moves forward into action during the invasion of France. The modifications of the Ausf.D variant gave it increased frontal armour, improved vision blocks for the driver, and a six-speed gearbox, which enhanced its cross-country performance. It was powered by a 250bhp Maybach HL 108 TR petrol engine and could reach a top road speed of 30kph (18mph). One of the most significant design features of this particular model was that its superstructure overhung the hull sides, allowing designers to up-gun the Panzer later in the war.

tank featured various modifications, including new suspension, gearbox and a hull letterbox mount for an MG34 machine gun. The new improved Panther immediately demonstrated its ability on the battlefield, and during one heavy tank battle in August 1943, the *Das Reich* Division managed to knock out 53 Russian tanks with its battalion of Panthers.

The success of the new improved Panther Ausf.D prompted the improvement of the Panther Ausf.A. Between August 1943 and June 1944, 1768 Panther Ausf.A were produced. During this period the Panther dominated the battlefield and soon great demands were put on it to fill the frontlines on both the Eastern and Western Fronts.

The final Panther variant to enter service was the Ausf.G, which was further modified with sloped instead of vertical armour on the lower-hull sides. It was also given additional armoured protection that was thickened to 5cm (1.97in). In total, there were 4185 Panther Ausf.G produced between 1944 and 1945.

In short, despite its problematic debut, the Panther was to go on and triumph over the majority of enemy tanks that came to confront it. On the Western Front it was superior to the Sherman, Churchill and Cromwell tanks. In the East it had the edge over its rival, the Soviet T-34/85. But it was difficult to manufacture and never available in adequate numbers to counter the high losses sustained on the battlefield.

Pz.Kpfw.VI Tiger I and King Tiger

Probably the most famous tank of World War II is the Pz.Kpfw.VI Tiger I. The Tiger I was built primarily in response to the heavy and powerful Soviet tanks like the KV I and II and T-34. From August 1942 to September 1944, when construction finally ceased, a total of 1354 Tigers left the production line. The Tiger I weighed and impressive 56 tonnes (55.1 tons). It possessed 10cm-thick (3.9in) frontal and 8cm (3.2in) side and rear armour. This massive machine mounted a lethal long-barrelled 8.8cm (3.46in) KwK 43 L/56 gun. The later version Tiger I had a 700bhp HL 230 engine, which could reach a maximum speed of 38kph (23.5mph) by road, and 20kph (12.5mph) cross-country. The first Tiger I to see action was deployed around Leningrad in August 1942. For the next two years the mighty Tiger I played a decisive role both on the Eastern and the Western Fronts. With its awesome killing power, it demonstrated its worth during the Citadel offensive, where it was distributed among the elite *Waffen-SS* Panzer units.

During 1944 the Tiger I played prominent roles in a number of major defensive battles that were fought against numerically superior Soviet forces. By mid-1944 however new heavy Russian tanks had begun to outclass the Tiger I and huge losses markedly reduced its effectiveness on the battlefields of the Eastern Front.

The Tiger I also made valuable contributions against Allied forces in northern France, where hundreds were deployed in the summer of 1944. The skill and tenacity shown by their crews there, together with the tank's killing power, made many Allied troops reluctant to engage the Tiger. It frequently took five British tanks to destroy one Tiger but despite its superb prowess, by early August 1944 the German front in Normandy was on the threshold of defeat. By late August most of the Tigers deployed in France had been destroyed.

Left: 1941, and the five-man crew of a Pz.Kpfw.IV Ausf.F1 clambers through their various allotted hatches to move off into action. The crew are members of the 6th Panzer Grenadier Regiment of the 7th Panzer Division. The Ausf.F1 variant was the first up-armoured vehicle developed in response to heavy Allied tanks during the Western Front campaign. It possessed homogenous armour plating that had been increased to 5cm (2.97in) thickness on all frontal surfaces and 3cm (1.18in) on the sides. By the time the German Army attacked the Soviet Union in June 1941, the *Panzerwaffe* fielded some 548 Pz.Kpfw.IV Ausf.F1 tanks.

ABOVE: On the Eastern Front, a Pz.Kpfw.IV Ausf.F1 moves through the undergrowth. Armed with a 7.5cm (2.95in) KwK 37 L/24, it was capable of dealing with Soviet KV-1 and T-34 tanks at short ranges only. When the Ausf.F2 went into production in March 1942, its new 7.5cm (2.95in) KwK 40 L/43 gun provided the technical superiority needed to combat the Russians.

With the heavy losses of the Tiger I, its production was terminated in favour of the superior King Tiger during September 1944. Like it predecessor, the Pz.Kpfw.VI Ausf.B King Tiger was a formidable tank and possessed lethal firepower. It was armed with a fearsome, long-barrelled 8.8cm (3.46) KwK 43/3 L/71 gun and for close defence also carried two MG34 machine guns. This massive behemoth weighed a staggering 69.4 tonnes (68.3 tons) and came with superb surrounding armoured protection, which rendered it virtually impregnable to any type of Allied attack.

The Henschel factory built 489 King Tigers by March 1945, including 20 command variants. Despite all its prowess and killing power however, the Tiger's enormous weight and huge fuel consumption rendered it slow and lacking in mobility. Consequently, it was used mainly in a static fire-support role. On the battlefield the King Tiger was a rare sight and peak usage only occured in February 1945 when 219 of them were fielded for operations with a few independent heavy tank battalions.

In December 1944, 52 King Tigers were used in the Ardennes offensive. However, their restricted mobility, especially across heavily wooded terrain, meant that they nearly always ran out of fuel, with the crew forced to bale out and fight on foot when ammunition would eventually run out. Despite this lack of mobility and its huge fuel consumption, the King Tiger scored a number of great tactical successes both on the Eastern and Western fronts. However, the failure on the Vistula Front and Ardennes left the crews of the King Tiger tanks battle-weary. Though they continued to fight with courage and zeal, they were unable to stave off the inevitable German defeat.

ABOVE: April 1941, the Balkans – two Pz.Kpfw.IIIs and a Pz.Kpfw.II have attempted to cross this fast-flowing river, but their weight has caused their tracks to sink into the bottom of the riverbed. The crews have obviously underestimated the river, a mistake that has cost them at least two of the tanks. In most cases, the crew can easily bale out, but under battle conditions such an error could cost the lives of the entire crew. Several Panzers that saw action both in the Balkans had, in fact, been specially waterproofed for the projected invasion of the British Isles in 1940, although these tanks obviously were not.

RIGHT: Another view of the Panzers that have succumbed to a fast-flowing Balkan river. The water has now risen up to the 3.7cm (1.45in) gun barrel and will soon engulf both vehicles. Tanks were versatile machines and many had waterproofed engines that allowed them to wade across rivers and streams without much hindrance. However, if the water managed to find its way into the engine compartment, there was a good chance that it would stall, and any prospect of re-starting was impossible unless the tank could be extracted and moved to dry ground.

RIGHT: September 1942, west of Stalingrad – a photograph taken from the command hatch of a Pz.Kpw.III Ausf.H. To the left is a Pz.Kpfw.IV Ausf.F1 armed with a 7.5cm (2.95in) KwK 37 L/24 gun. On the right is a Pz.Kpfw.III Ausf.J equipped with the 5cm (1.97in) KwK 39 L/60 gun. With its more potent gun, the weight of the Pz.Kpfw.III increased to 22.3 tonnes (21.9 tons). Between March 1941 and July 1942, some 2516 of these Ausf.J variants were constructed. They saw widespread service on the Eastern Front and were a formidable adversary to the Soviet T-34 tanks at short ranges.

BELOW: Summer 1941, and a Pz.Kpfw.IV Ausf.F1 passes two Opel *Blitz* trucks that have been covered with foliage for extra camouflage. The Pz.Kpfw.IV has been given additional armoured protection by adding of track links to the front of the tank. Its commander is wearing the black Panzer uniform and *Feldmütze*. Of note is the Army marksmanship lanyard, reserved for troops of armoured units. The other two crewmembers are both wearing the one-piece boiler suit garment produced for armoured vehicle crews. It could be worn over the black Panzer clothing.

BELOW: On the Eastern Front a column of Pz.Kpfw.IIIs roll forward across the endless steppe. At the beginning of the invasion of Russia, many Panzer commanders considered themselves invincible, believing that the Soviet Union would fall quickly. Along the entire German front, the great armoured force would smash its way forward into action, deployed in extended order of advance and stretching over a distance of 11–16km (7–10 miles). By the end of the first day of battle, the leading Panzer divisions would be well clear of the fighting zone and have advanced further afield.

LEFT: Spring 1942, southern Russia – standing inside a medium cross-country Horch staff car, a *Gebirgsjäger* officer from the 1st Mountain Division passes an armoured column of the 1st Panzer Army. The command pennant attached to the bumper of thecar indicates the car belongs to a Panzer division. To the officer's right is a stationary Pz.Kpfw.IV Ausf.F1. In the spring of 1942, the 1st Mountain Division fought as part of the 1st Panzer Army in the area of Donetsk. During the summer, it spearheaded the drive into the Caucasus and remained there until 1943.

ABOVE: A Pz.Bef.Wg.III. advances across the vast sprawling expanse of the Russian steppe. In the distance a railway line has come under heavy aerial attack, bringing a Soviet locomotive to a burning halt. This command tank is armed with a 3.7cm (1.45in) gun mounted in the turret and an MG 34 mounted beside it for self-defence. This particular vehicle is still finished in its original dark grey base and carries the tactical number '6' painted in white on the turret rear.

ABOVE: April 1941, and a group of old men and children are captivated by the arrival of some German armour inside their town. These vehicles belong to the 46th Panzer Corps, which has temporarily halted its furious advance on Belgrade but by 12 April the Corps had captured the city. The Panzer in the foreground is a Pz.Kpfw.III equipped with a 3.7cm (1.45in) gun. Behind the tank is an Sd.Kfz.251 halftrack with frame antenna. This *Kommandopanzerwagen* is a specialized command vehicle intended for senior commanders. It incorporated office facilities, cypher and encoding devices, and several radios.

ABOVE: Early April 1941, and a Pz.Kpfw.IV from the 46th Panzer Corps drives towards Belgrade. This corps was opposed mainly by Croats, who were no match for the superior might of the *Panzerwaffe*. The main body of the 46th Panzer Corps entered Belgrade on 12 April, while another Panzer division from this corps simultaneously occupied Zagreb. The following day, on 13 April, the 46th Panzer corps rolled forward to Sarajevo, breaking the last organized enemy resistance.

RIGHT: July 1943, and during the battle for Kursk a Pz.Kpfw.III. Ausf.J sits in a field with other variants, preparing to move off into action. This particular model is armed with the long 5cm (1.97in) KwK 39 L/60 gun, and is also fitted with *Schürzen* to protect it from anti-tank fire. The Pz.Kpfw.III made a critical contribution to the enormous successes achieved during the first two years of the campaign on the Eastern Front.

ABOVE: Summer 1941, Russia – laden with Panzer troops, Pz.Kpfw.IIIs and other vehicles roll along a dusty road. The armoured divisions were dependent upon the Russian roads but, ironically, the problem was less the absence of good roads than the fact that they found it difficult to conceal themselves. A typical Panzer division could cover an area of some 28.5 square kilometres (11 square miles) throwing up huge clouds of dust in the process, which consequently could reveal the division's position to a Soviet fighter-bomber flying above.

BELOW: July 1943, the battle for Kursk – a Pz.Bef.Wg.III.Ausf.J command tank, its 5cm (1.97in) gun barrel removed, wades across a stream. The vehicle has intact side skirts, indicating that it has not seen many heavy confrontations. This is a regimental staff vehicle: its first tactical number painted in red on the side of the turret is marked with a letter 'R'. The Panzer is painted in overall dark sand and has a camouflage scheme of thin green and brown wavy lines. Both crew members are still wearing the, by now, old black Panzer uniform with black *Feldmütze*.

ABOVE: Summer 1943 – a group of Pz.Kpfw.IV Ausf.H from the 3rd SS-Panzergrenadier Division *Totenkopf*. The Pz.Kpfw.IV Ausf.H was equipped with a potent KwK 40 L/48 gun, and had two 7.92mm (0.31in) MG 34 machine guns as secondary armament. This variant incorporated further improvements, including the added protection of 8cm (3.15in) of hull nose armour, which increased its weight to 25 tonnes (24.6 tons). This powerful variant dominated the *Waffen-SS* and was used extensively in the *Totenkopf* division. At Kursk the *Totenkopf* played a prominent role.

LEFT: Summer 1941, and the crew of a Pz.Kpfw.IV Ausf.F1 pose for the camera. On the left mudguard, the letter 'K' indicates that the tank is attached to *Panzergruppe Kleist*. During this early stage of the war, Panzer crews were still wearing their famous black Panzer uniforms. However, they soon realized that the uniform was completely unsuitable for camouflage purposes.

BELOW: Late November 1942, Stalingrad – a Pz.Kpfw.III. Ausf.J crosses a prefabricated bridge. By this period of the battle for the city, General Paulus's 6th Army was close to being encircled and cut off. For days, debilitated Panzer crews struggled on in vain, trying to regroup their precious Panzers and protect them from the pulverizing effects of enemy anti-tank fire and snipers.

LEFT: Tripoli, North Africa and a column of Pz.Kpfw.IIIs equipped with 3.7cm (1.45in) guns roll through the city. The robust and reliable Pz.Kpfw.III was used extensively in North Africa and formed the backbone of the Panzer divisions in the desert during 1941. These tanks belong to the 5th Panzer Division, which was ordered by Rommel to drive round the block to give the impression that a large army had docked. By early March 1941, the Panzer force had struck eastwards, quickly and decisively, to drive the British from back their strongholds.

ABOVE: A column of Pz.Kpfw.IIIs rumbles through the town of Tripoli in February 1941. These tanks belonged to the 5th Panzer Division. Despite this grand display of military might, General Rommel was aware that his Panzer force was still not strong enough to penetrate the strong British lines. In order to dupe the enemy into believing that his forces were too strong for them to attack, he decided to have dummy tanks constructed. Rommel wrote: 'To enable us to appear as strong as possible and to include maximum caution in the British, I had the workshops three miles south of Tripoli produce large numbers of dummy tanks, which were mounted on Volkswagen and were deceptively like the original.'

ABOVE: A group of Pz.Kpfw.IIIs have halted in the desert during operations in North Africa in 1942. The crew of one Panzer are captivated by the appearance of a Ju 87 *Stuka* dive-bomber. The Ju 87 *Stuka* was used extensively in North Africa to dive-bomb and strafe in order to seek out enemy artillery units and pave the way for armour. Out in the desert the Germans used *Blitzkrieg* tactics and deployed armour, motorized infantry and air power in coordinated attacks for rapid penetration.

BELOW: Even in the desert propaganda was used to maximum effect and here a Pz.Kpfw.III passes a cameraman. During the war Rommel's mighty Panzer force in North Africa featured regularly in the newspapers, newsreel reports and on various propaganda posters. Propaganda newsreels made much of the tank men, showing the soldiers to great effect in their black uniforms or denim overalls moving across conquered terrain with an aura of invincibility.

ABOVE: During the battle of Kursk, a flamethrower-equipped Pz.Kpfw.III tank from the *Grossdeutschland* Division clears Soviet defensive lines in front of a fortified village. The main objective of Operation Citadel was the destruction of the Red Army's massive force in the Kursk region. Once the Soviet Army had been destroyed, the German Army could then turn north and drive on to Moscow. Despite the huge resources poured into the battle and the new tanks that rolled off the assembly lines onto the battlefield in July 1943, the *Panzerwaffe* was unable to overcome the Soviet tanks and artillery.

RIGHT: Beside a road in southern Russia, a Pz.Kpfw.III armed with a 3.7cm (1.45in) gun is stationary in front of an Opel *Blitz* truck. The tank formed part of the 1st Panzer Army in the Donetsk area and the soldiers belong to the 1st Mountain Division. This tank is probably attached to *Panzerjäger Abteilung* 54, which was one of the main constituent units of the 1st Mountain Division. This unit took part in the defensive battles in southern Russia, after the debacle at Stalingrad, until March 1943.

ABOVE: Italy 1943, and a Pz.Kpfw.IV. Ausf.F2 from an unknown Panzer division is on the road to Bitonto. The Ausf.F2 variant mounted the more powerful long-barrelled 7.5cm (2.95in) KwK 40 L/43 gun. This new L/43 made the tank a more potent tank than its predecessors, and proved its worth against the American and British tanks that invaded Italy that summer. The gun possessed a muzzle velocity of 740m/s (2428ft/s), which allowed it to penetrate 8.9cm (3.5in) of sloped armour at 1000m (3282ft). The vehicle's weight was increased to 23.6 tonnes (23.2 tons), which reduced its top speed to 40kph (25mph).

ABOVE: Northern Italy, and a Panzer crew are camouflaging their old Pz.Kpfw.IV. One of the most effective forms of protecting a tank from anti-tank fire and also from aerial recognition was to bury the vehicle up to its tracks and lay foliage over its turret. The tactical number '121' has been painted on the side of the turret. The tactical numbering system chosen for Panzers was simple: the first numeral indicated the company, the second the platoon (*Zug*) within the company, and the third the vehicle within the platoon. Thus '121' meant: 1st company, 2nd platoon, 1st tank in the platoon.

ABOVE: During a temporary lull in the fighting at Kursk, the crew of a Pz.Kpfw.III make minor repairs to their vehicle. At the battle of Kursk, seven Panzer divisions in total were smashed, with catastrophic effect on the German war effort. The defeat was so severe that General Heinz Guderian feared the *Panzerwaffe* would never be able to recover to defend against the steadily advancing Red Army.

BELOW: July 1943, and a group of Pz.Kpfw.IV Ausf.J move forward during Operation Citadel. The Pz.Kpfw.IV with side-skirt armour also carries a line of steel helmets on the back of the engine deck. This was a relatively common procedure, and various forms of additional armoured protection were used, including track links, metal plating, tank wheels, jerry cans, metal buckets and even concrete.

RIGHT: July 1943, and a Pz.Kpfw.IV Ausf.G halts during its advance through the Kursk salient. This vehicle still carries the old 1940 divisional sign for the 4th Panzer Division – painted in yellow to the right of the MG 34 machine gun. On the side of the turret, also painted in yellow, is the standing bear, the emblem of the 4th Panzer Division. During the Battle of Kursk, the 4th Panzer Division lost nearly 50 per cent of its Panzer force. After Kursk, the division was a shadow of its former self. In February 1944 the division became heavily embroiled in action to relieve Kovel, where the German garrison had been encircled. It took the division, supported by the 5th SS Panzer Division *Wiking* and a few other units, two months to break through the Soviet lines and enter Kovel.

LEFT: Another view of the Pz.Kpfw.IV Ausf.G. The standing bear emblem can clearly be seen to the right of the tactical number '420'. These particular Ausf.G variants featured enhanced armour protection and an improved muzzle brake on the main armament. During its long production run, some 1724 of them were built, a longer 7.5cm (2.95in) L/48 gun being introduced from late 1942. By 10 July 1943 the German front at Kursk was collapsing all around the 4th Panzer Division, forcing individual units to fend for themselves as they retreated from the Red Army. As German armour slowly gave ground, pitch battles were fought for control of roads against strong Soviet defensive positions and armoured spearheads.

ABOVE: The crew of a Pz.Kpfw.IV Ausf.H are busy cleaning equipment. One of them has made use the *Zeltbahn* as a makeshift teepee. On the tank, the regimental standing bear emblem is painted in white and the new divisional emblem has been applied on the turret side skirt, a black shield with old divisional emblem and other markings in yellow. The vehicle is painted in overall dark sand with a very light camouflage pattern of green patches. The muzzle brake has been covered to protect it against particles entering the barrel.

BELOW: This Pz.Kpfw.IV belongs to the 4th Panzer Division; the vehicle retains its old 1940 divisional emblem painted in yellow on the turret side skirt. The tactical number '505' has also received a yellow coat of paint. The tank has received a coating of anti-magnetic mine paste, or *Zimmerit*. The sole purpose of *Zimmerit* was to protect the steel surface from magnetic anti-tank grenades. Based on nitro-solvents, *Zimmerit* was rippled to increase thickness and thereby surface distance from the steel, without increasing the weight of the coating.

LEFT: July 1943, and during the Battle of Kursk, Panzer grenadiers hitch a lift on board a Pz.Kpfw.IV. The vehicles protective side skirts are still intact. They were made of mild steel plates 0.5cm (0.2in) thick and were designed to protect the tank from rounds fired at close range by Russian anti-tank rifles. The skirting was also very effective against hits from 7.5cm (0.2in) high-explosive shells. The steel skirting also provided protection against hollow charge projectiles by exploding the shells away from the vehicle.

ABOVE: 1943, northern Italy – a group of Panzergrenadiers take cover behind a Pz.Kpfw.IV. The protective covering over the muzzle brake suggests that the tank has been knocked out of action or abandoned by its crew, and is now being used as cover by the troops. Although the mountainous terrain of Italy prevented large-scale tank operations, the rugged terrain offered Panzer crew's good defensive positions. Along many of the defensive lines, they took full advantage and incorporated their machines into fixed emplacements to create formidable obstacles for the advancing Allied troops.

ABOVE: June 1944, Normandy – two British soldiers pose with a couple of French girls on top of a destroyed StuG.III Ausf.G assault gun. This final variant mounted a powerful 7.5cm (2.95in) StuK 40 L/48 gun. It was more than capable of penetrating up to 9.1cm (3.58in) of 30-degree sloped armour, and 10.9cm (4.3in) of unsloped armour from a distance of 100m (328ft). The Ausf.G was also the first variant to carry an MG 34 machine gun for local defence and it was also better protected than its predecessor, having 3cm (1.2in) thick appliqué plates bolted onto the hull front.

ABOVE: July 1943, and a Pz.Kpfw.IV takes action during Operation Citadel. Although this variant has no *Schürzen,* it does have turret side skirting. Scattered pieces of foliage have been crudely attached to the tank, in order to break up the shape of the vehicle. For the attack on the Kursk salient, all available armour was concentrated in two gigantic pincers – General Model with his 9th Army attacked from the north, and General Hoth with his 4th Panzer Army from the south. Hoth was given eight Panzer divisions and Model five. Virtually the entire operational reserve was flung into the offensive.

ABOVE: 22 June 1941, and a Pz.Kpfw.Ausf.F1 *Tauchpanzer* pushes forward along a sandy road after crossing the Bug river, near Patulin. The *Tauchpanzer* was a specially converted submersible Pz.Kpfw.IV and was originally designed for the invasion of the British Isles in 1940. Note the national flag draped on the rear of the tank for aerial recognition. During the latter part of the war, when the *Luftwaffe* had been all but destroyed, many Panzer crews avoided draping national flags across their vehicles, as they became easy prey to low-flying enemy aircraft.

RIGHT: Late 1943, and two Pz.Kpfw.IV Ausf.H shelter inside a Russian village not far from Velikye Luki. Both vehicles appear to be intact and have no signs of battle damage. The tanks have turret side skirts and there are also support brackets for *Schürzen,* indicating that the crew will soon be attaching them. By late 1943, German armour had been severely mauled on the Eastern Front. These two Pz.Kpfw.IVs are probably new Panzers, a rarity among the Panzer crews that drove them.

BELOW: Italy, 1943 – a Pz.Kpfw.IV being given directions by one of the crewmembers. The Italian campaign was fought over hilly, close terrain and Panzer crews found it very different from the fighting on the open steppes of the Eastern Front. It was not a terrain that suited tank warfare, but the Pz.Kpfw.IV with its potent 7.5cm (2.95in) gun defended the surrounding countryside with extensive fields of fire. However, by 1944 the lack of transport and logistic support was forcing the German Army to withdraw and unable to recover damaged vehicles from the battlefield.

RIGHT: August 1943, and after the futile and costly attacks at Kursk a column of intact Pz.Kpfw.IVs move west to a new defensive line. Crews of Pz.Kpfw.IVs found Operation Citadel frustrating at times: their tanks were not good enough to effect a breakthrough against a deep anti-tank front. Tanks fought in wedge formation, the *Panzerkeil,* which until the Kursk offensive had proved very successful against strong Russian anti-tank fire. The spearhead of the wedge was formed by the heaviest tanks, like the Tigers and Panthers, with the Pz.Kpfw.IVs following closely behind.

BELOW: 1943, Italy – a Pz.Kpfw.IV with turret skirting makes a sharp 90-degree turn to conceal itself under the protection of some trees. The crewmembers are wearing the later M1943 *Einheitsfeldmütze* field cap. Although these caps became increasingly popular during 1943, the peak of the cap prevented easy use of the periscope visor sights inside the tank. Crews therefore began wearing them back to front. The crews are also wearing the special lightweight green denim Panzer uniforms that were introduced to be worn by the men in hotter climates.

LEFT: A Pz.Kpfw.IV with intact *Schürzen* rolls through an Italian town. Apart from the driver, the rest of the crew are taking in the fresh air. When they were not in combat conditions, the crew almost invariably spent most of their time out of the claustrophobic and often thoroughly unpleasant environment of the interior of the tank. Even at the best of times, tanks were hot and stuffy, and in hotter climates the crews felt that they were being cooked alive. Sweating and choking, many tank crews served wearing only shorts and canvas shoes.

ABOVE: Somewhere on the Eastern Front, the crew of a Pz.Kpfw.VI Tiger.I are using a tree and the side of a house as protective cover. This massive 56-tonne (55.1-ton) Tiger I carried a five-man crew. It mounted a lethal long-barrelled 8.8cm (3.46in) KwK 43 L/56 gun and possessed 10cm (3.94in) frontal and 8cm (3.46in) side and rear armour. The Tiger played a prominent role in Russia, and was used with lethal effect during the Battle of Kursk in July 1943. There they demonstrated their awesome killing power, and wreaked death and carnage on anything that attempted to stop them.

RIGHT: An airfield in Russia, and this Pz.Kpfw.VI Tiger.I has smoke candle dischargers fitted on the turret. These were discontinued in June 1943. The absence of *Zimmerit* from this vehicle, which was applied to armoured vehicles only after September 1943, indicates that this is an early Tiger. Between August 1942 and September 1944, some 1354 Tiger Is were constructed. During this period, these vehicles demonstrated both the lethalness of their 8.8cm (3.46in) guns and their invulnerability against Soviet anti-tank shells.

ABOVE: November 1942, the Eastern Front – an early model of the Tiger I. A group of *Wehrmacht* soldiers surrounds the vehicle: this is most likely the first time they have seen a Tiger. The tank visibly carries no camouflage scheme and has not even received a winter whitewash. This early Tiger I is powered by a 642bhp Maybach HL 210 engine. With a potent 8.8cm (3½in) gun, it had secondary armament of two 7.92mm (0.312in) MG 34 – one co-axial in the turret and one mounted in the hull at the front. The first Tigers to see operational duty in Russia did so near Leningrad.

BELOW: A Pz.Kpfw.VI Ausf.E Tiger hurls along a road in broad daylight in Normandy, 1944. The Tiger I had already gained a superb fighting record on the Eastern Front, but here in northern France it contributed to some of the *Panzerwaffe's* most impressive exploits during the last year of the war. Despite Allied superiority and the damage inflicted on the Panzer divisions, the Tigers excelled in their defensive role. Their fire power created 'Tiger-phobia' among the Allied ranks, with British and American tank crews so wary of the powerful Tiger that they frequently refused to attack it.

ABOVE: On the Eastern Front, a Pz.Kpfw.VI.Tiger I equipped with an 8.8cm (3.46in) KwK 36 L/56 gun barrel. The later version Tiger carried a more powerful 700bhp Maybach HL 230 P45 V12-cylinder petrol engine. With a maximum weight of 56 tonnes (55.1 tons), it had a maximum road speed of 38kph (24mph) and a maximum cross-country speed of 20kph (12.5mph). Its 543-litre (118-gallon) fuel tank allowed it an operational road range of only 100km (62miles), and an operational cross-country range of 60km (37 miles).

BELOW: Normandy, France, just before the Allied invasion in 1944. A column of intact StuG.III Ausf.G assault guns from the Panzer regiment of the *SS Adolf Hitler Leibstandarte* Division. The Ausf.G was the last variant assault gun to enter service, and mounted a very powerful 7.5cm (2.95in) 40 L/48 gun. It was also the first variant to carry a MG 34 machine gun for local defence. The StuG.III Ausf.G remained operational with the *Waffen-SS* until the end of the war and was, in fact, the most common armoured fighting vehicle used.

ABOVE: Mid-April 1944 – a Pz.Kpfw.VI Tiger I Ausf.E of the *Schwere Heeres Panzer Abteilung 507* near Tarnopol, just after the city was captured. The 507th was formed in September 1943 and was equipped with 45 Tigers between December 1943 and February 1944. In March 1944 the 507th was transferred to the Eastern Front where, despite receiving 44 further replacement Tigers, it had lost all but seven by February 1945.

BELOW: A transport train loaded with vehicles of a Tiger I battalion heading for the Eastern Front just before the Russians launched Operation Bagration on 22 June 1944. The main factor in the success of the Panzer divisions in Russia was their ability to reach threatened sectors of the front swiftly. Travelling by rail was the quickest and easiest way to transport German armour, but it did render them vulnerable to aerial attack.

ABOVE: On the Eastern Front, the crew of a Tiger I rest and have a bite to eat while waiting for maintenance to their tank to be completed. All independent Tiger battalions were equipped with maintenance companies responsible for repairing and keeping the Tigers in working condition. The heavy armoured plating of the Tiger was more resistant to combat damage than other lighter tanks and with a well equipped maintenance company they could be returned to the battlefield to swiftly.

ABOVE: This photograph of a Pz.Kpfw.V Panther in Russia, 1943, from the *Großdeutschland* Division was probably taken near Rzhev during the summer. The division fought almost exclusively in the central and southern sectors of the Eastern Front and came to be known as 'Hitler's trouble-shooters', being deployed wherever the need was greatest. As at 20 June 1942, the organization of the Infantry Division (Motorized) *Großdeutschland* consisted of two infantry regiments, each of three battalions; a heavy weapons battalion; and one tank battalion with three companies, made up of 30 Pz.Kpfw.IVs.

BELOW: March 1944, and out on the frozen Russian steppe a group of Panthers and a solitary Pz.Kpw.IV prepare to move into action. Snow has settled on their hull fronts, affording the tanks some camouflage protection in the arctic surroundings. The Panther Ausf.D was powered by a large 700bhp Maybach HL 230 V12-cylinder petrol engine and a more resilient AK 7-200 gearbox than its predecessor. It had a potent long-barrelled 7.5cm (2.95in) KwK L/70 gun. From February 1944, German factories welded 0.5cm (0.2in) skirt plates onto all existing Ausf.D Panthers.

ABOVE: December 1944, Poland – this Pz.Kpfw.V Panther has been painted with white winter camouflage paint, including its side skirts. The tank weighed 44.8 tonnes (44 tons) and had a maximum road speed of 46kph (29mph). It maximum cross-country speed was 30kph (19mph). With a fuel capacity of 730 litres (161 gallons), the Panther had an operational road range of 200km (124 miles) and an operational cross-country range of 130km (81 miles).

ABOVE: Mid-July 1943, and in the early evening a column of Pz.Kpfw.IIIs push on along a dusty road, following the futile and costly defeat at Kursk. These vehicles belong to the 3rd Panzer Division. From 12–13 July 1943, the 3rd Panzer Division fought fiercely for the village of Beresowka, but was compelled to give up the village and surrounding areas due to stubborn Russian armoured resistance. Too weak to stem the Red Army onslaught, the Panzer division was driven west with huge losses. For the Panzer crews in the 3rd Panzer Division, the Russian counter-attack, with its masses of men and material, came as an unpleasant surprise.

RIGHT: Early January 1945, Belgium – Panzergrenadiers hitch a ride on board a Panther. This vehicle has clearly been embroiled in combat, for it has lost some of its *Schürzen* plates. By this period of the war, the *Panzerwaffe*, in spite of massive losses, continued to put up a formidable defence against both the advancing Red Army on the Eastern Front and the Allies on the Western Front. This photograph shows the Panther on the retreat during the later stages of the costly Ardennes offensive. During a period of one month's combat in the Ardennes, General Model's forces lost almost 600 armoured vehicles, including 190 Panthers and 120,000 soldiers, none of which could be replaced.

RIGHT: The crew of a well-camouflaged Panther load the tanks 7.5cm (2.95in) ammunition through the rear of the turret hatch, which also served as the crew's escape hatch. In total, 82 rounds of ammunition could be stored and 4200 secondary rounds. The 7.5cm (2.95in) KwK 42 L/70 gun that fired these shells was a very potent weapon indeed. It was extremely effective and quite capable of first-time hits at ranges over 1000m (3280ft). Its armour penetration capabilities were equally impressive. Its standard round was the Pzgr 39/42 armour-piercing ballistic capped with explosive filler and tracer. The pointed ends of these shells were designed primarily to reduce air resistance in flight.

BELOW: Photographed in the summer of 1941, a Panzer crew have pressed a Soviet T-34 tank into action. The vehicle retains a winter whitewash. Throughout the war, a number of captured enemy tanks were used by the German Army. Most were T-34s, T-60s and a few KV-1 and KV-2 tanks. To avoid friendly fire (all too possible, for obvious reasons), the Germans drew special attention to them and painted national crosses on them. Although the use of captured vehicles helped bolster the huge losses sustained by the Panzer divisions, some of the vehicles proved technically unreliable and finding spare parts was always a problem.

CHAPTER THREE

Light Tanks

Early German Armour

For the lack of a viable alternative, light tanks provided the main armour for the Panzer divisions during the early campaigns of the war.

Pz.Kpfw.I

The Pz.Kpfw.I, was the first light training Panzer built for the *Panzerwaffe* in 1934. Both the Ausf.A and the Ausf.B variants featured a machine-gun armed turret. The vehicle weighed 5.4 tonnes (5.3 tons) and it was armed with a 7.92mm (0.31in) gun. The tank also carried two radios, the Fu2 and Fu6. The Ausf.A was powered by a Krupp M305 engine that generated 57hp. The Ausf.B was slightly heavier and was fitted with a Maybach NL38TR 6-cylinder 100hp engine.

The Pz.Kpfw.I first saw combat during the Spanish Civil War. Between 1936 and 1938, 100 experimented in the art of *Blitzkrieg*. Following the Spanish Civil War, it was immediately recognized that the tank did not have any real combat potential. However, this still did not prevent the German Army equipping its *Panzerwaffe* with 1445 Pz.Kpfw.Is for the Polish campaign in 1939. Once again the Polish war taught a valuable lesson, namely that the Pz.Kpfw.I was under-gunned and under-armoured and

would not be able to fight effectively against heavier and superior enemy tanks. Nonetheless, Hitler's military ambitions forced the *Panzerwaffe* to use more than 1400 of them during the campaign in the West. Once again, superior German battlefield tactics overcame the inferiority in numbers of her armoured force. A year later the unsuitable Pz.Kpfw.I saw limited action in North Africa, and was also deployed to fight during the opening stages of the Russian campaign in 1941.

By early 1942 the Pz.Kpfw.I was taken out of service and given to the police and anti-partisan units. They were also used for training purposes and were an excellent training tank. In fact the majority of the Panzer crews were trained on the Pz.Kpfw.I until the end of the war.

LEFT: A cannibalized Pz.Kpfw.II somewhere on the Eastern Front. This vehicle once belonged to the 9th Panzer Division, as indicated by the divisional tactical sign painted in yellow on the side of the turret left of the number '4'. This light Panzer weighed 8.9 tonnes (8.8 tons) and mounted a 2cm (0.79in) KwK 30 L/55 gun as its main armament. It was powered by a 140bhp Maybach HL 62 TRM engine.

LEFT: August 1941, Russia – a Pz.Kpfw.38(t) moves along a dusty road. This Czech-built tank is equipped with a 3.7cm (1.46in) KwK 38(t) L/47.8 gun and has two 7.92mm (0.31in) MG 37(t) guns for local defence. Some 400 of these vehicles were manufactured in eight different variants. The later models were up-armoured and a few were rearmed with the German-made 3.7cm (1.46in) KwK 35/36 L/46.5 gun. The Pz.Kpfw.38(t) saw extensive service during the early part of the war but the ever increasing need to replenish the Panzer divisions with heavier armour meant that by 1942 the Pz.Kpfw.38(t) had been relegated to second-line duties.

Pz.Kpfw.II

Until the Pz.Kpfw.III and IV entered service, German factories were ordered to mass-produce the Pz.Kpfw.II Ausf.A. This light Panzer weighed 8.9 tonnes (8.8 tons), and mounted a 2cm (0.79in) KwK 30 L/55 gun as its main armament. It was powered by a 140bhp Maybach HL62 TRM engine. During 1937 to 1939, four variants were built, the Ausf.B, Ausf.C, Ausf.D and Ausf.E. A total of 1226 Pz.Kpfw.II were employed for the Polish campaign, and the following year more than 1000 were fielded for the invasion of the West. Large numbers of the Pz.Kpfw.II

ABOVE: France 1940, and a group of Pz.Kpfw.38(t)s from General Rommel's 7th Panzer Division attack French forward positions. The Pz.Kpfw.38(t) saw widespread action during the invasion of France and matched the majority of Allied tanks both in speed and fire power. However, even during this early period of the war the 38(t) was no more than a stopgap, providing the *Panzerwaffe* with an alternative to the Pz.Kpfw.III, which was slow in arriving in good numbers.

were also used in North Africa and in the opening phases of the invasion of the Soviet Union. However, despite its extensive use between 1939 and 1941, the tank was undoubtedly under-gunned and suffered from very thin armour, which offered minimal protection in battle. Despite its ineffectiveness on the front lines, production of the Pz.Kpfw.II continued with the manufacture of the Ausf.F, Ausf.G and Ausf.J types. The Ausf.F featured a homogenous 3.5cm-thick (1.38in) frontal plate, and side armour was increased to 3cm (1.18in). One of the rarest vehicles in the *Panzerwaffe* was the Pz.Kpfw.II Ausf.L *Luchs*, or Lynx. Only 100 of these vehicles were ever manufactured and they were distributed between the 4th and 9th Panzer divisions. Section and platoon leaders' vehicles were fitted with FuG12 radio set and star antenna. The rest were equipped with the FuG Spr.Ger.f.

Although the Pz.Kpfw.II was never to be used extensively again after 1941, a number of units, including the *Waffen-SS*, found use for it as a reconnaissance vehicle during late 1942 and early 1943. Starting February 1943 the tank began to be phased out and withdrawn from operational duties. Consequently all the Pz.Kpfw.II were withdrawn from frontline service by the end of 1943. However, a great number of them were subsequently converted into the *Marder* light tank destroyers, and *Wespe* self-propelled howitzers.

Pz.Kpfw.38(t)

The German occupation of Czechoslovakia meant that in March 1939, German tank designers were able to capture 150 Czech LT-38s that were still in production and complete them. All of the machines were soon incorporated in the *Panzerwaffe* as Pz.Kpfw.38(t) Ausf.A. Following the German capture of Czechoslovakia, the LT-38 became the most important tanks used by the *Panzertruppe* and it remained in production as a battle tank until mid-1942.

The Pz.Kpfw.38(t) Ausf.A weighed 9.6 tonnes (9.4 tons) and was powered by a Praga EPA 6-cylinder 125bhp engine. Its main armament was a 3.7cm (1.45in) KwK 38(t) L/47.8 gun and had two 7.92mm (0.31in) MG37(t) guns for local defence. Approximately 1400

RIGHT: November 1941, Russia – two Pz.Befw.38(t)s can be seen moving forward in support of advancing infantry. The leading tank is a command vehicle, or a *Panzerbefehlswagen 38(t)*, as is identified by the frame antenna that has been bolted on its engine deck and by the tactical number painted in white on the side of its fixed turret. By this period of the war, the 38(t) was steadily loosing increasing numbers on the Eastern Front. Under-gunned and under-armoured, its effectiveness was very limited and they were no match against the mighty Soviet T-34 tanks.

Pz.Kpfw.38(t)s were manufactured in 8 different variants, the Ausf.A to Ausf.F and two later types, the Ausf.S and Ausf.G. The later models were up-armoured and a few rearmed with the German-made 3.7cm (1.45in) KwK 35/36 L/46.5 gun. A number of them were also converted into flamethrower tanks by replacing the hull machine gun with a flamethrower.

The Pz.Kpfw.38(t) saw extensive service during the early years of the war in Poland, the Low Countries, France, the Balkans and even on the Eastern Front, during the first few months of the invasion of Russia. However, the tank was far too under-armoured and under-gunned, and its usefulness, particularly against Russian tank, was very limited. The ever increasing demand to replenish the *Panzerwaffe* with heavier armour eventually relegated the Pz.Kpfw.38(t) to second-line duties by 1942.

By this period, in response to decreasing armour on the Eastern Front, designers began the usual process of adapting the chassis for other purposes and up-gunning the fire capabilities of the old machines. The first conversion of the Pz.Kpfw.38(t) commenced with the *Marder III* and *Flakpanzer* 38(t). During 1942 and 1943, the Pz.Kpfw.38(t) had its turrets removed and was converted to driver training vehicles based on turretless tanks; these were then designated Pz.Kpfw.38(t) *Schulfahrwanne*. Various other conversions were also made, including a fast/light reconnaissance vehicle, ammunition and howitzer carrier and a command tank.

LEFT: Early November 1941, and these armoured vehicles are part of Army Group Centre, on parade on a frozen Russian steppe west of Moscow. The vehicle nearest the camera is an early production Sd.Kfz.263 radio vehicle. This armoured radio vehicle was equipped with a long-range radio set and was used by signal units and in corps and army headquarters. The Sd.Kfz.263 was open-topped and carried no armament. The vehicle was clearly distinguishable by its eight wheels and its antennae frame.

ABOVE: A Pz.Kpfw.I Ausf.B during the invasion of France. The Pz.Kpfw.I light tank was used extensively during both the French and Polish campaigns. The vehicle was armed with a ball-mounted machine gun for local defence. The tank also carried two radios, the Fu2 and Fu6. It was powered by a Maybach NL38TR 6-cylinder 100hp engine. Action in France demonstrated just how under-gunned and under-armoured the tank was – unable to fight heavier enemy tanks.

LEFT: 1940, the invasion of France – a muzzle brake of an unidentified gun barrel pounds positions forward of two Panzers. A preliminary bombardment of the objective area was an important prelude to a tank attack: screening the flanks of the attack with smoke and neutralizing the enemy's infantry in the rear areas was imperative. Terrain that offered insufficient cover was saturated by heavy shelling, enabling the Panzers to cross with the greatest possible speed.

ABOVE: Early November 1941, and the frozen steppe provides the ground for an armoured parade. A number of Pz.Kpfw.I Ausf.Bs pass a line of Panzer troops, including regimental bandsmen and trumpeters. One of the tank men acts as a standard-bearer and holds the regiment's standard. The crews are all wearing the old-style black Panzer beret, or *Schutmütze*. Although the Pz.Kpfw.II was used extensively on the Eastern Front, it was ineffective against superior enemy tanks and was phased out and withdrawn from operational duties by 1943.

BELOW: Summer 1941, and a group of Pz.Kpfw.38(t)s are being transported during the early phases of the Russian campaign. They are being ferried across a river using just the parts of a pontoon bridge. The usual procedure for crossing was that light vehicles were taken across first on rubber boats, and a pontoon bridge was then constructed for heavier vehicles. However, here the first available pontoons are being utilized as barges to ferry the Panzers, suggesting that the armour is needed desperately. Provisions are carried on the tank engine decks.

RIGHT: A column of Pz.Kpfw.I Ausf.As move along a dusty road in North Africa in 1941. The tanks are still in their old dark grey colour and have not been painted in overall dark sand. These vehicles belong to the 5th Light Division (later called the 21st Panzer Division). By 4 March 1941, General Johannes Streich, commander of 5th Light Division, had reached Mugtaa and was battering British forces into retreat. Within a month, the Panzers launched a three-pronged all-out assault, smashing their way across the open desert of Cyrenaica as they headed for Tobruk.

BELOW: A Pz.Kpfw.III passes a destroyed vehicle following intensive fighting out in the western desert in 1942. The tank has been given a liberal application of yellow paint – the colour of sand – which the Germans found to be the best method of camouflage to render their vehicles less visible in the desert.

Another form of concealment in North Africa – which also prevented unauthorized persons gaining battlefield intelligence regarding the identification of units and movement of troops – was the steady discontinuation of visible vehicle markings with unit designations.

ABOVE: Late winter 1942, Russia, a *Waffen-SS* crewmember stands on the deck of a whitewashed Pz.Kpfw.III.Ausf.J as it hurtles through the snow. The Ausf.J variant was the first tank to enter widespread frontline service with the *Waffen-SS.* During the spring and summer of 1942, the Germans added Panzer battalions to the SS Motorized Divisions *Wiking* and *Das Reich,* equipped with the Ausf.J variant. The first few hundred were still equipped with the 5cm (2in) KwK L/42 gun, but featured 5cm (1.97in) homogenous frontal armour. Subsequent Ausf.J variants featured the 5cm (1.97in) KwK 39 L/60 gun.

ABOVE: Summer 1941, Russia – and Panzers of Army Group Centre move towards their objective area during the rapid advance east. A Pz.Kpfw.38(t) leads the column, with two Pz.Kpfw.IV.Ausf.F1s following closely behind. At the outset of the invasion of the Soviet Union, the Panzer divisions drove deep into Russian territory, achieving unprecedented success against a demoralized and broken army. However, German armoured might was powerless against the primitive nature of the Russian road system. Had the Soviets built a road system comparable to that of their invaders, Stalin's army would probably have been defeated long before the autumn. Instead, the German mechanized forces, which had based their mobility on wheels instead of tracks, were compelled to travel on roads totally unsuited to this type of traffic.

LEFT: During the invasion of France, General Erwin Rommel sits in an open field, talking with members of his staff. Behind Rommel, officers, tank crews and other members of the armoured column belonging to the 7th Panzer Division rest in the long grass, surrounded by assorted vehicles – a Pz.Kpfw.38(t), a BMW R75 motorcycle combination, and an Opel *Blitz* truck. It was here that Rommel's legendary status increased as, over the course of just nineteen days, his Panzer division blazed across the Belgian and French countrysides at breakneck speed.

ABOVE: A Pz.Kpfw.38(t) rolls forward in 1940 during the invasion of France. This vehicle was used extensively during the campaign and was regarded by its crews as a reliable and effective weapon. Little consideration had gone into the design of the fighting compartment, but the commander-gunner had plenty of room and with ammunition in the turret he could easily load the 3.7cm (1.46in) gun. The Pz.Kpfw.38(t) dealt with both French and British tanks, but a year later on the Eastern Front came the first encounters with the T-34, and it was obvious that the days of this tank were numbered.

ABOVE: On the Eastern Front in 1941 the crew of a Pz.Kpfw.38(t) have just spent a number of hours resting prior to beginning another day's advance. The three-man crew have plenty of provisions stored on the rear deck of the tank and two of them are securing them down ready for the drive. The commander, dressed in his black panzer uniform, has a pair of vehicle uniform trousers in his hand. Of interest is the 3.7cm (1.45in) gun, which has been protected by specially tailored canvas sheeting, which was used primarily for keeping the barrel clean when it was not in use.

ABOVE: A Pz.Kpfw.38(t) belonging to *Panzergruppen Kleist*, which has been dug in beneath a tree, breaks cover, during the invasion of France in 1940. Of the 2702 tanks fielded against the British and French, there were 264 Pz.Kpfw.38(t)s distributed among the 10 Panzer divisions. *Panzergruppen Kleist* was to carry out the main breakthrough operation on the Meuse, so it was given the army's total allocation of the Pz.Kpfw.35(t) and 38(t) vehicles, the *Panzerwaffe's* best light tanks.

RIGHT: A Pz.Kpfw.35(t) rolls through a village during the Polish campaign in 1939. The Pz.Kpfw.35(t)'s armament, similar to the Pz.Kpfw.III, consisted of a 3.7cm (1.46in) gun and co-axial 7.92mm (0.31in) machine gun, with a further machine gun in the front plate. The vehicle saw use in Poland, France, Romania and Bulgaria, and later on the Eastern Front, but it was unable to cope with the harsh Russian winter, which rendered its pneumatic transmission inoperable.

ABOVE: A Pz.Kpfw.35(t) advances along a dusty road in Poland in September 1939. The Pz.Kpfw.35(t) was powered by a 125hp Praga EPA six-cylinder water-cooled engine. On later models of this light tank, the engine was fitted with twin carburettors, which raised the output power to 150hp. Ninety rounds of 3.7cm (1.45in) and 2700 rounds of machine gun ammunition could be stowed inside the tank, with the majority kept in the turret rear. This light tank had a four man crew: a commander/gunner, loader, driver and hull gunner/operator. The commander was located on the left of the turret beneath a rudimentary cupola incorporating four episcopes and a one-piece circular hatch.

ABOVE: One of the crew members of a Pz.Kpfw.38(t) in Russia, 1941, dismounts from his vehicle. The old divisional tactical sign painted in white on the front left, next to the antennae, indicates that it belongs to the 4th Panzer Division. This division saw extensive operations on the Eastern Front and was attached to the cutting edge of Army Group Centre, *Panzergruppe II*, commanded by General Heinz Guderian. For the invasion of Russia, a total of 623 Pz.Kpfw.38(t)s were fielded against the Red Army.

BELOW: Russian tanks in 1941 are first laid to waste, and subsequently smashed to pieces as the thundering Panzers reap a harvest of death and destruction. But even as German mechanized forces plunged ever deeper into Russia, scoring sizable successes along the way, the Soviets were already beginning to supply their forces with vast numbers of the new T-34 and KV-I tanks. They, coupled with the harsh Russian winter to come, would provide the Germans with their biggest test yet. The tide was about to turn.

CHAPTER FOUR

Assault Guns and Tank Destroyers

Mobile Fire Support and Enemy Tank Hunters

Assault guns and tank destroyers were first created in response to urgent demands for guns able to counter formidable Soviet armour. They were a valuable contribution and provided vital support for the troops in battle.

StuG.III

The origins of the assault guns, or *Sturmgeschütz*, initially lay in German artillery demands for an armoured vehicle that had armour piercing and high explosive capabilities and could provide attacking infantry fire support. In 1939 the *Sturmgeschütz* rolled off the prodction line. It was armed with a 7.5cm (2.95in) KwK L/24 gun and was installed in a fixed superstructure on the chassis of a Pz.Kpfw.III tank. The StuG.III Ausf.A was powered by a 300bhp Maybach HL120 TRM V12-cylinder petrol engine, which had a maximum road speed of 45kph (28mph) and a maximum cross-country speed of 19kph (12mph). Since the *Sturmgeschütz* was primarily designed as a close support weapon for infantry, this speed, especially across country, was deemed more than fast enough.

It was not until the spring of 1940 that a series of production models underwent a number of gruelling trials with five army batteries, one of them actually participating in the campaign on the Western Front in 1940. Later that year another StuG variant entered service, the Ausf.B, and the following year in 1941, some 548 further assault guns – the Ausf.C, Ausf.D and the Ausf.E variants – were built. All these types were

LEFT: On the Eastern Front in 1942, the commander of a StuG.III assault gun poses for the camera. This assault gun with the tactical number '131' has been up-armoured and re-armed with a longer-barrelled 7.5cm (2.95in) StuK 40 L/43 cannon to give it genuine anti-tank capability.

FAR LEFT: Infantry train with the support of a *Sturmgeschütz*, or StuG.III.Ausf.A assault gun in 1940. The soldiers are training in the art of tank co-operation, and the StuG.III proved to be valuable infantry support.

primarily constructed to be used on the Eastern Front, and were incorporated into special assault gun batteries, both for the army and their *Waffen-SS* counterparts.

During the first weeks of the invasion of Russia, the StuG.III performed well in an infantry support role. However, role was threatened by the appearance of growing numbers of heavy Soviet armour. The StuG.III was continually called upon for offensive and defensive fire support, where it was gradually compelled to operate increasingly in an anti-tank role. Subsequently, by late 1941, Hitler ordered that the StuG.III be up-gunned and up-armoured with a longer more potent 7.5cm (2.95in) gun, which would give it a genuine anti-tank capability.

This more powerful assault gun went into production in mid-1942 as the StuG.III Ausf.F. The vehicle mounted a longer 7.5cm (2.95in) StuK 40 L/43 gun and saw extensive action on the Eastern Front. The following year in 1943, the final StuG variant, the Ausf.G, came off the production line and rushed straight into service. It was armed with a 7.5cm (2.95in) StuK 40 L/48 gun and also carried for local defence, a 7.92mm (0.3in) MG34 machine gun.

By 1943 the StuG.III had become a very common assault gun on the battlefield, some 3041 of them becoming operational that year. A further 4973 StuG vehicles entered service between 1944 and 1945. The StuG had initially provided crucial mobile fire support to the infantry, and it also proved its worth as an invaluable anti-tank vehicle. It was at Kursk in July 1943 that it showed its true capabilities as a tank killer. In one tank battle a *Waffen-SS* assault gun battalion destroyed 129 Soviet tanks for the loss of just two assault guns. A year later the StuG also provided excellent service during the Ardennes offensive, where it spearheaded the first promising attacks. However, despite its proven tank-killing potential and its service on the battlefield both in offensive and defensive roles, the increased use of the StuG as a anti-tank weapon deprived the infantry of the fire support for which the assault gun was originally built.

TANK HUNTERS AND DESTROYERS

As the German Army plunged ever deeper into the Soviet Union during 1941, its forces soon found itself meeting ever stiffer opposition, including heavier and more powerful modern Soviet armour. In order to meet this growing threat and to prevent their front lines being smashed and overrun by Russian counter-thrusts, German forces eagerly called for more mobile anti-tank weapons.

In direct response, a number of improvised tank hunters were developed, which carried the most lethal anti-tank weapons the Germans had at their disposal. The development of the *Marder.III Panzerjäger* was the first of a series of improvised light tank hunters. Built on the chassis of Pz.Kpfw.38(t) and armed with a captured Soviet 7.62cm (2.95in) M36 field gun, the *Marder.III* quickly earned respect on the battlefield, and was more than capable of destroying the Soviet T-34 at normal combat ranges. With the success of the *Marder.III* came the development of a similar vehicle that was armed with a potent 7.5cm (2.95in) Pak 40/3 L/46 anti-tank gun. Utilising the Pz.Kpfw.38(t) Ausf.H chassis, armaments factories produced 418 of these vehicles between 1942 and 1943. By 1944 a new modified version, the *Marder.III* Ausf.M, entered service, and a total of 975 were built.

Throughout its service during the war, the *Marder.III* was an effective mobile anti-tank weapon that was always on hand to provide infantry anti-tank support. Although

ABOVE: Two StuG.IIIs supported by infantry advance along a dirt road in Russia in 1941. Designed primarily as an infantry support vehicle, the StuG.III had a fierce reputation. For the invasion of Russia, German factories were able to complete 548 StuG.III vehicles. The self-propelled assault gun had a crew of four and came equipped with a 7.5cm (2.95in) StuK 37 L/24 gun capable of traversing from 12.5 degrees left to 12.5 degrees right. It was powered by a 300bhp Maybach HL 120 TRM V12-cylinder petrol engine and had a maximum road speed of 45kph (28mph) and a maximum cross-country speed of 19kph (12mph).

ABOVE: A StuG.III.Ausf.E in Russia in 1941 has developed a mechanical problem after attempting an amphibious crossing. The StuG. III did have amphibious capabilities, but these were limited. Three crewmembers have opened the engine cover and are trying to locate where the water is causing the problem. Note that the vehicle's hatch has been protected by canvas sheeting. The StuG.III assault gun was a very robust, reliable and effective weapon.

the vehicle was vulnerable to enemy fire, it proved a valuable weapon against the growing might of Soviet armour. From 1942, it continued to serve in the front lines. A *Marder.II* was also constructed on the old Pz.Kpfw.II Ausf.D and Ausf.E chassis, and was armed with a 7.62cm (3in) gun. Later conversions also saw them carrying 7.5cm (2.95in) Pak 40/2 anti-tank guns.

The success of the *Marder.II* and *III* also saw the development of the *Marder.I*. The *Panzerjäger*, armed witha a 7.5cm (2.95in) gun, was converted from captured models of the French, fully-tracked *Lorraine* carrier. In total, 185 of these distinctive French boxlike open-topped vehicles were converted and entered into service. Though only lightly armoured, they were still a very powerful weapon, being used by some of the most elite formations in the German army on the Western Front in 1944. Despite the fact that these vehicles were eventually phased out during 1944 for a new generation, all-purpose tank destroyer, the *Marder.I*, *II* and *III* continued to serve Army and *Waffen-SS* anti-tank battalions.

The tank destroyer that was intended to replace the *Marder* was the *Jagdpanzer.38(t) Hetzer*. This would

become one of the most advanced tank destroyers of the war. Carrying a modified 7.5cm (2.95in) Pak 39 L/48 gun on a specially widened Pz.Kpfw.38(t) chassis, this destroyer, with its distinctive silhouetted armoured superstructure, entered production in 1944. By the summer of that year, it began to join the anti-tank battalions and saw action until the end of the war.

During 1944 another tank destroyer went into mass production with an improved version of the StuG.III assault gun – the *Jadgpanzer.IV* tank destroyer, nicknamed Guderian's Duck. The final variant of this machine, Pz.Kpfw.IV/70 came into service in late 1944. Armed with a 7.5cm (2.95in) StuK 42 L/70 gun, it proved capable of dealing with some of the heaviest Soviet armour.

Another rare tank destroyer to come out of production during the later part of the war was the *Jadgpanther*. Only 382 of these 45.5-tonne (50.2-ton) vehicles were ever built. These were very powerful tanks destroyers and were armed with an 8.8cm (3.46in) PaK 43/3 L/71 gun. They were embroiled in some of the heaviest fighting of the war and fought a bitter and defensive action until the very end of the war.

RIGHT: Summer 1942, Russia – an Assault Gun Battery is accompanied by Panzergrenadiers. The close formation of these assault guns suggests that the *Luftwaffe* have already attained complete air supremacy. Throughout the war, the *Sturmgeschütz* crews never regarded themselves as tank men. Rather, they were artillerymen who just happened to be manning mobile assault guns. Gradually, though, every crewmember came to respect and love his assault gun: in battle, crews were protected against direct infantry fire and felt impervious to anything except direct anti-tank fire.

BELOW: On the Eastern Front on October 1941 a group of soldiers take cover at the rear of a StuG.III. It appears that the soldiers have spotted enemy aircraft activity, for one of the men is actually hiding beneath the vehicle. A national flag has been draped over the engine deck for aerial recognition (to avoid incidents of 'friendly' fire). The StuG.III acquitted itself very well in its first actions in Russia. However, the lack of a machine gun for close support against enemy infantry was a problem with early variants. By September 1941, this was rectified by the introduction of the machine gun mounted on the Ausf.E.

ABOVE: A StuG.III Ausf.A in 1940 is put through its paces during a series of trials just prior to the invasion of the West. For the soldiers that were about to be plunged into action against the mighty French and British forces, the development of a piece of mobile artillery that could fight alongside infantry, as well as keep pace with the lightening advances of *Blitzkrieg,* was most welcome.

BELOW: A StuG.III passes a column of horse-drawn transport in southern Russia in the summer of 1941. Although the *Panzerwaffe* was to continue with its relentless drive through Russia, by late 1941 the prevalence of Soviet heavy armour demanded that the StuG.III be employed in an anti-tank role. Inevitably this deprived grenadiers of the fire support that the StuG.III was originally meant to provide.

ABOVE: Southern Russia in the summer of 1942. A soldier is stowing away his flamethrower equipment on board the rear of the StuG.III assault gun. The vehicle soon came under increased demand as the war progressed. It was used not only to carry troops into action and support them while in combat, but also to carry a whole variety of supplies and equipment that were needed to sustain the troops on the battlefield. By 1943, the paucity of transport meant that many StuGs and other self-propelled guns and tanks were compelled to carry more and more supplies.

RIGHT: A StuG.III ploughs through some undergrowth during the Balkan campaign in April 1941. Despite a number of minor problems with the StuG.III prior to the invasion of Russia, the experience of the Balkan campaign showed that that the assault gun provided the hard-fighting infantry with valuable support. Nowhere was this better illustrated than at Mount Ochiron, where the 72nd Infantry Division was supported by the first battery of Assault Gun Unit 191 at the Greek Metaxas Line. Between 1941 and 1944, the StuG.III was used extensively in Russia in this role.

BELOW: A cannibalized StuG.III. Ausf.B. Although this early variant proved a valuable support weapon to the infantry, its short 7.5cm (2.95in) gun could penetrate only 4cm (1.57in) of 30-degree armour at 1000m (3282ft). This vehicle has been fitted with the 7.5cm (2.95in) StuK 37 L/24 gun, which was installed in the early PzKpfw.IV medium tank. The letter 'A', painted in white on the side of the vehicle, indicates that this is the first gun in the battery.

BELOW: A StuG.III on the Eastern Front moves forward behind a long column in the summer of 1942. The vehicle carried a varied quantity of high explosive, smoke and armour-piercing rounds. During the first year on the Eastern Front, the assault gun proved indispensable to infantrymen and elite *Waffen-SS* formations alike. The development of this all-purpose built mobile assault gun exacted a deadly toll on enemy armour and was particularly successful supporting the infantry.

LEFT: A rear view of an unidentified armoured self-propelled StuG.III variant in southern Russia in 1942. Planning ahead for any eventualities, the vehicle can bee seen carrying logs on the engine deck, probably to be used if should the weather turn and muddy gravel is encountered. The vehicle needed to be capable of maintaining mobility, particularly off road, and ready to deal with any situation. Here, in the difficult mountainous terrains of the Caucasus, maintaining close cooperation between the infantry and the assault guns was crucial.

ABOVE: An early variant StuG.III moves through a German town in late 1940. The experience gained from the successful French campaign resulted in numerous service reports that were soon followed by initial orders for the further expansion in numbers of these assault guns. With its heavy armour and great off-road capability, the StuG (unlike the guns of the division's artillery) could follow the infantry of the *Panzertruppen* everywhere. Its main tasks were to suppress heavy infantry and anti-tank weapons that could not be destroyed by heavy infantry weapons.

ABOVE: A StuG.III follows closely in support of the attacking infantry. The StuG is equipped with a 7.5cm (2.95in) StuK 37 L/25 gun. The assault gun posseses 5cm (1.97in) of thick frontal armour and 4.3cm (1.7in) of side armour, providing it with protection superior to that of any of its contemporary tanks. With its low silhouette for better survivability, it not only provided sterling offensive service, but fought brilliantly during defensive battles as well.

RIGHT: A rare photograph showing a group of Bulgarian soldiers supported by a StuG.III in the Balkans in August 1944. During that period the Germans sent a substantial quantity of armour to the area in an attempt to defend from the advancing Red Army. Eighty-eight Pz.Kpfw.IVs and fifty assault guns were placed at the disposal of the Bulgarian Army. Hitler felt compeled to use them as a reserve force against the Soviets and even grudgingly declared them the most reliable of the Balkan allies on the strength of their hatred of the Greeks and fear of the Turks.

BELOW: Late summer, 1944, and on the Eastern Front a StuG.III.Ausf.G has halted along a dirt track. The crew are talking to a group of grenadiers. Foliage has been heavily applied over the hull of the vehicle to break up the shape of the assault gun and prevent being discovered from the air by the Soviet fighters that had by this stage of the war total control of the skies. For the German armoured forces, Russian air power was the most dangerous opponent they faced. When travelling, virtually all armoured vehicles were camouflaged with branches and other pieces of foliage to avoid aerial detection.

ABOVE: Early 1945, and in western Germany a StuG.III.Ausf.G rolls forward towards the front lines. Once again, heavy foliage has been applied over the assault gun to camouflage it from the increasing menace of Allied aircraft. The vehicle has obviously been embroiled in some heavy combat, as it has lost five of its six *Schürzen* plates. By this period of the war, StuG vehicles and their crews were suffering heavy losses, and this MG 34 machine gun has been mounted with a special metal shield. By 1945, it was not uncommon to attach concrete to the roofs of some assault guns as additional protection.

RIGHT: June 1944, Normandy – just a few days after the successful Allied invasion of Europe. A British soldier poses for the camera, sitting proudly on top of a knocked-out StuG.III.Ausf.G in an unidentified French village. With ever more serious tank shortages, German factories increased the production of assault guns. In December 1944, when Hitler unleashed his Ardennes offensive, the StuG.III spearheaded the German armoured assault across Belgium towards the American lines. Even during the last months of the war, the StuG.III assault guns remained the most common fighting armoured vehicle in the *Waffen-SS*.

LEFT: Most like;ly taken in 1940, during the invasion of France, this photograph shows the *Panzerwaffe's* first tracked tank destroyer, a Sfl auf Pz.Kpfw.I.Ausf.B assault gun. The chassis has been converted to mount the gun; this vehicle was fitted with a Czech PaK 4.7cm (1.8in)(t) anti-tank gun as standard. The mounting for this weapon was protected on three sides by armour plate and provided a limited traverse of fifteen degrees. A total of 86 rounds of ammunition could be stowed, and a crew of three was carried. The gun remained in service unti 1942.

ABOVE: July 1943, and the crew of a *Marder.III Panzerjäger* pose for the camera. The *Marder. III* was the first of a series of improvised light tank hunters, and was built on the chassis of a Pz.Kpfw.38(t). This particular vehicle is fitted with a captured 7.62cm (3in) Russian Model 36 anti-tank gun. The vehicle also had a travel lock on the front of the hull to secure the huge barrel while travelling long distances. Some 418 of these light tank hunters were produced in 1942. A newer variant, the *Marder.III.Ausf.M*, remained in production until May 1944, and a total of 975 were built.

LEFT: Mid-1943, and a *Marder.III Panzerjäger* rolls along a Russian road. It was powered by an 125 bhp Praga EPA TZJ R6-cylinder petrol engine and had a maximum road speed of 42kph (26mph) and a maximum cross-country speed of 24kph (15mph). The *Marder.III* was an effecive weapon and provided both the *Wehrmacht* and *Waffen-SS* with the mobile anti-tank capability they needed.

BELOW: Winter 1944, the Ardennes – a StuG.III.Ausf.G, equipped with the 7.5cm (2.95in) StuK 40 L/48 gun. An application of *Zimmerit* anti-magnetic paste can clearly be seen. These vehicles were very popular during the Ardennes offensive due to the assault gun's low silhouette and its good fuel economy, which made it an obvious choice for operations in such hilly terrain.

LEFT: German soldiers boarding a StuG.III Ausf.G in Normandy in June 1944. An MG42 machine gun is visible on the roof of the assault gun. The StuG was extensively used during the battle of Normandy. No less than 1673 tanks and assault guns were distrbuted among nine Panzer divisions in France in 1944, but by the the end of the summer campaigns the majority of these vehicles had been lost. Despite frantic attempts to fill the massively reduced ranks with replacement assault guns, they were not enough to prevent the allied onslaught.

ABOVE: Somewhere in Russia, three Marder.IIIs, armed with captured Soviet anti-tank guns, cross a bridge. This vehicle had a lightly armoured, three-sided shield fitted directly onto the chassis. With no real form of protection from the elements, apart from the warmth radiating from the engine, the crew spent almost the whole winter cold and miserable. However, these vehicles proved valuable to the *Panzerwaffe* and were used to provide not only the *Waffen-SS* grenadiers with mobile anti-tank support but even the *Wehrmacht* with mobile artillery support on the front lines.

BELOW: France 1940, and a column of armoured vehicles, made up of the 15cm (5.9in) *Schweres Infanteriegeschütz* (sIG) 33 heavy infantry gun and halftracks, line the roadside. Although rare machines, two sIG 33 guns formed the heavy infantry gun platoon of SS grenadier and *Panzergrenadier* regiments from

1940 until the end of the war. The letter 'K' painted in white on the sIG 33 indicates that it belongs to *Panzergruppe Kleist*. The letter 'E' and the tactical numbers '706' means that this is the 4th gun of self-propelled Heavy Infantry Gun Company 706, which belonged to the 10th Panzer Division.

LEFT: A long column of StuG.III AusfGs advance along a frozen road during the winter of 1944. The StuG.IIIs have received a coating of winter whitewash and have all intact side skirts, indicating that they have not been embroiled in heavy combat. The StuG.IIIs are armed with the long-barrelled 7.5cm (2.95in) StuK 40 L43 cannon, which delivered an almighty punch. In additon to the main armament the assault gun carries the 7.92mm (0.31in) MG34 machine gun for local defence. Between 1944 and 1945 some 4973 StuG.III AusfGs were produced.

RIGHT: Trundling along a dusty road during the Balkans campaign is a sIG 33 heavy infantry gun belonging to '704' Gun Company of the 5th Panzer Division. The canvas sheeting attached to the front of the vehicle's shield has in all likelihood been put up by the crew to protect the gun and keep dust and dirt out of the gun and fighting compartment. In the weeks and months leading up to the invasion of Russia, the *Panzerwaffe* carefully built up their assault forces, utilizing all available reserves and resources. During the Russian campaign a number of sIG 33 heavy infantry guns saw active service, but gradually most of the guns of this type disappeared. Only the 5th Panzer Division kept some of these machines in active service until the summer of 1943.

LEFT: Early August 1944, and a Stumpanzer IV. Ausf.J, also called *Brummbär*, stands inside the city of Warsaw. The vehicle's main armament is a 15cm (5.9in) StuH 43 L/12 short-barrelled gun. A total of 306 of the *Brummbär* were built during the war. The first variants consisted of 52 new Pz.Kpfw.IV.Ausf.E and F, with doubled 10cm (3.94in) front armour, 6cm (2.36in) on the sides and a shutter to provide an observation slit for the driver, but not the machine gunner. The later variants, the Ausf.H and J, were equipped with a 7.92mm (0.312in) MG 34 machine gun in a ball mount with *Schürzen*. The *Schürzen* fitted to the vehicle was 0.5cm (0.2in) mild steel boilerplate attached by brackets to protect the hull against hollow-charge weapons.

RIGHT: 1943, Italy – another *Sturmpanzer* IV.Ausf.F prepares for action. This *Brummbär* lacks the mounted MG 34 standard on later variants. The driver's observation slit is covered and has a periscope for safer viewing. The 15cm (5.9in) StuH 43 L/12 short-barrelled gun was a very potent weapon and saw action at Kursk in July 1943. The first unit equipped with the *Sturmpanzer* at Kursk was the Assault Tank Battalion 216. It was generally a reliable vehicle, and although it was heavy and slow, this did not prove a real problem as its intended role was providing heavy fire against fixed positions at the forefront of an infantry assault.

BELOW: July 1943, Kursk – and a sIG 33 auf Fgst Pz.Kpfw.38(t) *Bison* Ausf.M hurtles along a road towards the front lines. This vehicle was armed with a powerful 15cm (5.9in) gun barrel. On the basis of its chassis, the *Bison* was basically a member of the *Marder* family, which profited from the Pz.Kpfw.38(t). In a firing position, the crew had a panoramic telescope projected above the side armour. This vehicle has been heavily camouflaged. In open country, to protect themselves against being spotted by Soviet aircraft, the crew had to do all they could to camouflage their large guns.

CHAPTER FIVE

Artillery

Guns of Destruction

Artillery support was crucial for armoured attack and provided much firepower needed to sustain the German Army in both defensive and offensive roles.

SELF-PROPELLED GUNS

In 1942 the German armed forces realized that one of the major weaknesses within the structure of the Panzer divisions was the severe lack of self-propelled artillery. The development of a new batch of self-propelled guns was therefore considered imperative. From the designers' blueprints came two self-propelled guns that remained the backbone of the German armoured artillery until the end of the war, the *Wespe* and *Hummel*.

Production of the *Wespe* began in 1942. It was armed with a 10.5cm (4.13in) light field howitzer in an open-topped, boxlike superstructure built on top of a Pz.Kpfw.II chassis. Powered by a Maybach HL62 engine, it had a maximum road speed of 40kph (25mph) and managed 20kph (12mph) cross-country. Between 1942 and 1944, some 683 *Wespe* self-propelled guns left the factories for operational duties. The Wespe remained the most frequently built German self-propelled light howitzer during the war as designers were unable to create a more viable model.

Another self-propelled gun that was almost as popular as the *Wespe* and also made its debut in 1942 was the *Hummel*, or 'Bumble-Bee'. This very effective weapon

LEFT: Summer 1942 in the Caucasus, a *Wespe* self-propelled artillery gun of the 1st SS Panzer Artillery Regiment of 5th SS Division *Wiking* passes a destroyed T-34. The *Wespe* was armed with a 10.5cm (4.1in) leFH 18/2 L/28 gun. Powered by a Maybach HL62 engine, it had a maximum road speed of 40kph (25mph), and managed 20kph (12mph) cross-country.

mounted a standard 15cm (5.9in) heavy field howitzer atop the Pz.Kpfw.III/IV chassis. From the time the first *Hummel* left production in December 1942 until the program was finally terminated in late 1944, a total of 666 *Hummel* self-propelled guns were built.

Both the Russians and their Western Allies were concerned by the devastating impact of the German self-propelled guns, which was first felt at the time Citadel was unleashed in July 1943. Despite their small numbers, for the next two years of the war these two self-propelled guns scored sizable successes on both fronts. However, by mid-1944 the Allied bombing campaigns were causing severe problems, and shortages of fuel and spare parts were crippling the Panzer divisions in which they served. By the end of the war, only a handful of *Wespe* and *Hummel* machines were captured intact.

ANTI-TANK AND FLAK GUNS

During the Second World War the German Army had a variety of anti-tank weapons at their disposal. These weapons included anti-tank guns, anti-tank mines, anti-tank rockets and anti-tank rifles. The first anti-tank gun to serve in the German Army at the start of the war in 1939 was the 3.7cm (1.45in) Pak 35/36. The Germans fielded some 11,200 Pak 35/36 anti-tank guns in Poland, where the gun proved more than adequate against the lightly armoured opposition. However, it was in France in 1940 that the German Army encountered heavy Allied armour

LEFT: Summer 1941 on the Eastern Front. A 15cm (5.9in) sFH18 heavy field howitzer hurls a shell against Russian positions. The gun had a maximum range of 13,250m (43,500ft). Artillery support was a prerequisite for a successful tank attack. Crews took great care not to hinder the momentum of the armoured attack and made sure that the heaviest fire fell well ahead of the tanks or even outside their sector.

ABOVE: South of Obojan on 5 July 1943, a *Wespe* self-propelled artillery gun belonging to the armoured artillery regiment of the *Großdeutschland* Division moves into position from the north. Despite the punch from its potent 10.5cm (4.13in) leFH 18/2 L/28 gun, the vehicle was only lightly protected, with 1cm (0.4in) armour on the superstructure and 1.8cm (0.7in) on the hull. The large gun mounted on the small chassis limited ammunition stowage to a maximum of 32 rounds.

ABOVE: During Operation Citadel in July 1943 a well camouflaged *Wespe* battery fords a shallow stream. The *Wespe* was thinly armoured to offset the added weight of the gun and, like all self-propelled gun mounts, had open hulls that offered little protection for the men and guns. This was a result of operational requirements – the need to be able to follow the tank for long distances, alter direction quickly and be ready to fire again immediately without delay.

and soon came to appreciate the tactical limitations of its small anti-tank gun. After the Western campaign, the Army concluded that it desperately needed a heavier anti-tank gun. On the Eastern Front the following year, the Army learned just how ineffective the Pak 35/36 had become, especially against the new Soviet T-34 and KV-tanks. Despite various modifications to the gun's performance, it was still not enough to hold back the growing armoured might of the Soviet Army. Subsequently, new anti-tank weapons were built, including the 5cm (1.97in) Pak 38, the 7.5cm (2.95in) Pak 40 and the potent 8.8cm (3.46in) Pak 43, which was the most lethal anti-tank gun to see operational service during the later part of the war.

Another weapon used extensively against the Soviet Army was the flak gun. The first flak gun to see service was the 2cm (0.79in) Flak 30, which saw action in Poland in 1939. Following the Polish campaign, the gun was improved and the 2cm (0.79in) Flak 38 entered service. Although the Flak 38 was a formidable weapon, the most famous German anti-aircraft gun was the heavy Flak 88. After a number of improvements in 1941, the gun became a very important weapon to the *Panzertruppen*, as it was specifically designed for a dual role, one that included a very lethal anti-tank capability. Firing armour-piercing rounds, it could unleash one of its shells and pierce 13.2cm (5.2in) of armour at 2000m (6567ft). Throughout the war it demonstrated its outstanding anti-tank capabilities and became a very popular weapon among the flak units it served.

Other useful flak weapons used during the war were those mounted on the back of halftrack artillery tractors. The first mobile flak guns to be mounted in such a way were produced after the Polish campaign, where a number of 2cm (0.79in) self-propelled anti-aircraft guns were fixed on board Sd.Kfz.10 halftrack artillery tractors. By 1942 various flak guns were mounted on the back of the artillery tractors, with the most popular being the 3.7cm (1.45in) Flak 36 that was mounted on an Sd.Kfz.7 halftrack. Even Opel *Blitz* trucks and various other vehicles were modified to use flak guns.

ARTILLERY

Providing massive firepower support in both defensive and offensive roles, artillery included field, mountain and light, plus howitzers. It was primarily the artillery regiments that were given the task of destroying enemy positions and fortified defences and of conducting counter-battery fire prior to an armoured assault. Employment of artillery was a necessity to any ground force engaging an enemy. Both infantry and motorized artillery regiments became the backbone of the army and paved the way for the Panzer divisions to pour through and achieve their first tactical successes. Once a tank attack was in progress, the artillery would move forward with the first wave and continue to pour harassing fire where enemy anti-tank weapons, tanks and artillery were located or suspected.

The most widely used piece of artillery during the war was the 10.5cm (4.13in) *leichte Feldhaubitze 18* (leFH 18), or light field howitzer. More than 5000 were in service by the time war broke out in 1939. Later in the war, the leFH 18 was modified and fitted with a muzzle brake and a more powerful propellant charge. However, it soon proved too heavy and cumbersome, so in 1941 the Germans fitted the howitzer's barrel to the carriage of the 7.5cm (2.95in) Pak 40 anti-tank gun.

Another artillery piece to see extensive use, until the end of the war, was the 15cm (5.9in) sFH 18 heavy field howitzer. It provided support not only to the advancing

troops, but also to those retreating from the Eastern Front, when it gave reliable support in defending against continuous Red Army attacks from all sides. Initially the heavy sFH 18 howitzer was horse-drawn, but this was considered awkward and time-consuming. Gradually the gun was towed almost exclusively by prime mover where it was generally transported in two pieces.

Various other field guns were also employed for action on the front lines. These included the 7.5cm (2.95in) light field gun and 7.5cm (2.95in) *Geb 36* mountain gun that was employed in both artillery and an anti-tank role. A rarer weapon to see action was the 10cm (3.93in) *schwere Kanone 18*, 18/40 and 40 heavy gun. Another piece of artillery to enter service was the 10.5cm (4.13in) *GebH 40*, and became the standard German mountain howitzer of the war. One of the largest calibre pieces to see action was the 21cm (8.25in) *Mörser 18* (Mrs 18), which was capable of firing to a maximum range of 28,000m (91,086ft).

ABOVE: A *Wespe* is preparing to fire against Russian positions in 1943. The crewmember can be noted looking through his binoculars, deducing the exact location of the enemy to order the gunner to adjust the correct distance and height required to fire the gun. The *Wespe* was the most common German self-propelled light howitzer of the war.

ABOVE: Passing a group of Russian peasants, a *Wespe* advances towards the front lines. The driver's hatch is open. The barrel of the gun, cradle and pneumatic recuperator ran through a simple slit in the angled front plate, but was moved backward to leave the driver's compartment unaffected and give the driver a clearer view. The *Wespe* had good off-road capability, but still required a certain amount of skill to manoeuvre as the gun was nose-heavy, which made steering difficult at times.

ABOVE: An Sd.Kfz.10/4 halftrack clears a forest area to allow the crew to set up a temporary position under the protection of some trees. The vehicle is equipped with a 3.7cm (1.46in) Flak 38 anti-aircraft gun, mounted on the back of the halftrack. On board, space for the crew was at a premium. In action, as can be seen here, the side of the gun platform could be folded down to provide additional space for the crew to manoeuvre around the gun. Magazines for the gun were carried in ready racks on the folding sides of the platform. Some of the vehicles also carried a single axial trailer with additional ammunition.

RIGHT: A battery of *Wespe* self-propelled guns opens fire simultaneously during a defensive action in Poland late summer 1944. Both of the vehicles' guns can be seen recoiling. The sound of these 10.5cm (4.13in) guns in action can be easily imagined as witnessed by the number of men holding their ears. The *Wespe* and *Hummel* were introduced in the spring of 1943 and soon became the backbone of the Panzer artillery. Between 1942 and 1944, some 683 *Wespe* self-propelled guns left the factories for operational duties, mainly on the Eastern Front.

ABOVE: During Operation Citadel in July 1943 a *Wespe* crew have elevated their gun barrel to the firing position. For the next two years until the end of the war, the *Wespe* remained a reliable, tested weapon that gave good service in all combat situations. Within their 38 light armoured howitzer units, the Panzer divisions of the *Wehrmacht* had at least 76 batteries using these self-propelled guns, and a total of some 85 batteries, including armoured brigades and special units. Undoubtedly, the *Wespe* remained the best known and most important German self-propelled gun.

ABOVE: A *Hummel* is embroiled in action in Poland, January 1945. This heavy self-propelled gun possessed only 2cm (0.79in) of armour on the lower hull and 1cm (0.39in) on the superstructure – this was in order to limit the weight. By this period of the war, the Panzer divisions in the East had suffered massive casualties. Each Panzer division barely had the required strength of more than 100 tanks, with new ones denied to old formations being used instead to build up fresh divisions.

ABOVE: The fighting compartment of the *Hummel* self-propelled gun. The *Hummel*, or 'Bumble-Bee', mounted a standard 15cm (5.9in) heavy field howitzer in a lightly armoured rear-fighting compartment built on top of a Pz.Kpfw.III/IV tank chassis. This vehicle weighed a hefty 25.9 tonnes (23.5 tons), and to limit the weight the crew could carry only 18 15cm (5.9in) rounds at a time. In total, some 666 *Hummel* self-propelled guns were constructed for the war effort.

BELOW: A 10.5cm (4.13in) lFH 18 M L/28 on a GW 39 H (f) *Hotchkiss* chassis in Normandy, summer 1944. Sixty of these captured vehicles were rebuilt for artillery and were used solely in France. Re-fitted only due to pressure to get more armoured artillery onto the battlefield, they were heavy, complicated to operate and gave poor engine performance. Nonetheless, the crews that operated these captured vehicles were able to accomplish more than was expected of them.

ABOVE: 1940, and during the invasion of France, the crew of a 15cm (5.9in) sFH 18 field howitzer prepare to fire their gun at enemy positions. Before an armoured attack, artillery crews concentrated on enemy tanks in the assembly areas, unleashing their fire power where anti-tank units were suspected to be located. Artillery fire was heaviest on areas where Panzers would be unable to operate, but from where they could be engaged effectively. High explosives were also targeted against probable enemy observation posts to blind them with smoke.

BELOW: 1940, France – the field howitzer crew wait during a lull in the fighting. To break up the gun's shape, canvas sheeting has been draped over the left wheel. The spade trails have not been dug in, which suggests a rapid German advance. The mission of the artillery before an attack was to neutralize the opponent's anti-tank defence in the area between the line of contact and the regimental reserve line. Continuous counter-battery fire prevented the enemy from shelling the tank assembly area and breaking up the preparation of the attack.

RIGHT: Along the banks of the Dnieper River in Russia is a group of armoured vehicles and a heavy field howitzer belonging to the 4th Panzer Division. In early July 1941 the 4th Panzer Division broke through the 'Stalin Line' of fortifications and advanced at breakneck speed towards the Dnieper. By 4 July units of the division were ordered to take Staryi Bychoff and the bridge across the river. It was here that the division met strong Russian resistance. Although it successfully battered its way through to Propoisk, it was down to 25 operational tanks following a number of heavy tank battles.

BELOW: April 1941, the Balkans – a wide variety of armoured vehicles, including halftracks advance along a congested road. One halftrack is towing a 15cm (5.9in) sFH18 heavy field howitzer. When the German Army attacked the Balkans, the Yugoslavs found themselves overwhelmed. Only two-thirds of their 28 divisions and three cavalry brigades had been mobilized, and they lacked modern equipment, having no armour and only 300 antiquated machines.

RIGHT: On the Eastern Front in 1942 a ferocious artillery bombardment lights up the night sky. As an armoured attack progressed, heavy fire was maintained to engage successive lines of anti-tank defences. When the tank managed to break through the enemy forward defence lines, all the heaviest fire fell well ahead of the armoured assault or outside their sector. Every artillery commander was aware that the flanks of a tank attack were also vulnerable, so they assigned the artillery units the task of protecting the flanks by barrages of high explosive and smoke shells.

BELOW: June 1940, northern France — a 15cm (5.9in) sFH 18 heavy field howitzer sits under camouflage netting. The sheer power of this weapon could hurl its destructive charge up to 13,250m (43,500ft) away. As the standard heavy field howitzer in the *Wehrmacht,* the gun was very effective at clearing up heavily concentrated defensive positions to let tanks and infantry pour through unhindered. Much of the transportation of this howitzer was done by halftrack instead of horse. This enabled crews to work more effectively and minimized the distance between artillery and advanced Panzer units.

ABOVE: On the Eastern Front during the early phase of the campaign in 1941, a 10.5cm (4.13in) leFH 18 light field howitzer has been destroyed. This light field howitzer was the standard field piece of the light batteries. It weighed 1985kg (4377lb) and fired a 14.8kg (32.6lb) shell at a maximum velocity of 470m/s (1542 ft/s) to a maximum range of 10675m (35,025ft). In combat, these light howitzers proved too heavy, and as a consequence in 1941 the Germans fitted the howitzer's barrel to the carriage of the 7.5cm (2.95in) Pak 40 anti-tank gun to produce the leFH 18/40.

LEFT: October 1941, and the crew of a 15cm (5.9in) sFH 18 heavy field howitzer load one of the gun's 43.52kg (96lb) projectile into the breech to prepare the gun for action. Lots of foliage has been applied to the howitzer, including the spade trails. In a Panzer division there were usually three fully mechanized batteries in an artillery regiment. These included two batteries of 12 10.5cm (4.13in) howitzers, and one medium battery with one troop of four 10.5cm (4.13) guns and two of four 15cm (5.9in) gun howitzers.

BELOW: On the *Westwall*, or Siegfried Line on 15 April 1940 a 15cm (5.9in) sFH 18 heavy field howitzer barrel has just been loaded from the gun carriage trailer to the barrel trailer and is being pushed through the thick mud by the gun crew.

RIGHT: Three Sd.Kfz.10 gun tractors in Italy 1943. Two of the vehicles are towing a 7.5cm (2.95in) heavy anti-tank gun. These guns served both as artillery and in an anti-tank role. The Sd.Kfz.10 gun tractors were primarily used to tow guns and carry the crew. They were also modified to mount an entire 3.7cm (1.46in) PaK 35/36 anti-tank gun with shield on the rear of the tractor, facing forward so that the gun fired over the cab. As additional protection for the crew, some of these vehicles featured an armoured cab over the driver's compartment.

ABOVE: The Balkans campaign in April 1941. An Sd.Kfz.7 with a mounted four-barrelled light anti-aircraft gun has halted inside a town. The 2cm (0.79in) Flak 38 gun was first developed by the German Navy in 1940, but it was quickly introduced into the *Wehrmacht* and *Waffen-SS*. A very powerful quadruple mounted gun, it could fire a lethal 1800 rounds per minute, making it a deadly weapon not just against low flying aircraft, but also against ground targets.

ABOVE: During the Balkans campaign, a halftrack tows artillery and its crew. This vehicle belongs to the *Gebirgs-Artillerie Regiment* 79 of the 1st *Gebirgs*-Division. The division had performed with distinction during the invasion of France and the Low Countries in 1940, at the crossings of the Maas and Loire rivers, and then in 1941 it took part in the invasion of Yugoslavia. That summer, the 1st *Gebirgs*-Division also saw action in Russia in Army Group South and was involved in extensive operations at the Uman Pocket, Kiev, Stalino and at the crossing of the River Dnieper.

LEFT: Early June 1940, and a Pz.Kpfw.38(t) thunders past the crew of a 3.7cm (1.46in) Pak 35/36 during an attack on French positions. The crew of the gun appear to be screening the flanks of the armoured advance, protecting the attacking Panzers against enemy tanks. The Pak 35/36 became the standard anti-tank gun of the *Wehrmacht* and *Waffen-SS* during the early part of the war. It weighed only 432kg (952.5lb) and had a sloping splinter shield. The gun fired a solid shot round at a muzzle velocity of 762m/s (2500ft/s) to a maximum range of 4025m (13200ft).

ABOVE: An Opel *Blitz* truck tows a 3.7cm (1.46in) Pak 35/36 gun in northern France on June 1940. During the invasion of France, code-named Operation Red, the *Wehrmacht* and its *Waffen-SS* counterparts became aware of the tactical limitations of the Pak 35/36 as their forces increasingly encountered heavier enemy armour, such as the British Matilda and the French *Char B* tanks. To the worry of the German gunners, their 3.7cm (1.46in) shells simply bounced off these tanks' thick armour, even at point-blank range. The army quickly realized that it was in desperate need of acquiring more effective anti-tank weapons.

BELOW: Early summer 1942, and a *Gebirgsjäger* 3.7cm (1.46in) Pak 35/36 gun crew have just opened fire against an advancing Soviet tank. During the terrible fighting on the Eastern Front, the German Army quickly recognized the obsolescence of the Pak 35/36, which up to then had been mass-produced. When the invasion of Russia was unleashed, there were some 14,459 of the guns in service. However, they were no match against new Soviet armour like the T-34 and KV-1 tanks. To the crews' consternation, the rounds of the Pak 35/36 simply bounced off the frontal armour of the T-34s that engaged them.

LEFT: Somewhere on the Eastern Front, a gun crew of a Pak 35/36 opens fire along a road against Russian armour. Smoke indicates that there has probably been more than one impact from the shell. The gunner looking through his pair of binoculars is probably deducing the location and range of the target. Russian tanks too often tore into Pak 35/36 gun positions, causing many of the crews to abandon their guns in panic. As heavier anti-tank guns entered service during 1941–43, the Pak gun was increasingly relegated to foreign volunteer, training and security units.

ABOVE: An SdKfz.251 and an Sd.Kfz.7 towing a PaK 40 wade through a river in the Eastern Front to avoid a minefield. The 7.5cm (2.95in) PaK 40 was a heavy gun that was more than capable of firing a shell to a maximum range of 2000m (6560ft). It could penetrate 9.4cm (3.7in) of armour at 1000m (3280ft). In service it proved a powerful and deadly weapon.

RIGHT: During the build-up for the Kursk offensive in July 1943, a halftrack artillery tractor towing a Flak 88 gun passes a stationary *Elefant* self-propelled anti-tank gun on a muddy road in the Kursk salient. The *Elefant*, also known as the Ferdinand after its designer, Ferdinand Porsche, was based on the Tiger tank chassis. Armed with an 8.8cm (3.45in) gun, it lacked a machine gun for close-in defence against enemy infantry, and moved too slowly. It made its debut at Kursk but was a failure, and relatively few were made.

ABOVE: Early autumn on the Eastern Front and a gun crew are preparing to fire out on the vast Russian steppe. One of the gunners is about to look through the gun sight. This let him give the crew accurate information about the correct range and elevation needed to fire the gun. If the rounds fell short of the target, he could then advise them on the corrections needed to hit the target. All the crew are wearing the Model 1935 steel helmet except for the gunner looking through the sight who is wearing the Model 1938 *Feldmütze*.

BELOW: France in 1940. A converted 8-ton prime mover is equipped with a flak gun. This was a formidable, though (thankfully for the Allies) uncommon, improvised heavy anti-aircraft weapon. This 8.8cm (3.46in) Flak gun mounted on a swivel platform fired a 9.4kg (20.7lb) shell at a muzzle velocity of 795m/s (2609ft/s), firing armour-piercing rounds against ground and air targets. A fully equipped crew were capable of firing 15 rounds per minute and engaging targets at an altitude of up to 8000m (26245ft).

RIGHT: A well camouflaged 8.8cm (3.46in) Flak 41, in its elevated position, prepares to fire against enemy aircraft on the Eastern Front in in 1941. The 8.8cm (3.46in) heavy Flak 18 gun, or 'Flak 88', was perhaps the most famous German artillery gun of World War II. The gun was specifically designed for a dual-purpose role, possessing a very potent anti-tank capability as well. The gun had a slightly longer 71-calibre barrel, as compared with the older 56 calibre, and this gave it an increased muzzle velocity of 980m/s (3216ft/s) when firing armour-piercing rounds and a horizontal range of 20,000m (65615ft). The gun trailer can also be seen heavily camouflaged. Out on the Russian steppe armour was particularly vulnerable to enemy observation.

LEFT: A flak crew during a brief lull in the fighting in Russia in the summer of 1942. As heavier and more lethal Soviet armour was brought to bear against the Germans in 1942, *Wehrmacht* and *Waffen-SS* units clamoured to obtain more flak guns that could deal with increasing threat. During 1942 a number of divisions increased their anti-aircraft battalions, each of which contained two or even three heavy batteries. In some sectors of the front, some units had barely enough Panzers to oppose the Russian armour and called upon the flak battalions to halt the Red Army's relentless advance. During this period a number of flak guns came to be assigned dual purposes, which involved adding an anti-tank role to their operational duties.

RIGHT: A 'Flak 88' is elevated into the air, ready to fire against possible Russian aircraft in 1942. This flak gun proved to be a very reliable and versatile weapon, and it continued in production until the end of the war in 1945. It weighed 7800kg (17,199lb) and fired 20 rounds per minute. The letter 'D' painted in white indicates that it belongs to the fourth battery. Of interest is the number of kill rings on its 8.8cm (3.46in) barrel. Victory markings, either rings painted around the barrel of the gun, or silhouettes or symbols depicting the targets destroyed, was a widespread practice in German military units. They marked the number of enemy targets destroyed – whether aircraft, vehicles, or targets such as bridges, trains, buildings. One tank even suceeded in sinking a ship!

BELOW: Beside the banks of the Volga river in August 1942 a flak gun is fitted on a mounted trailer that was designed specifically for transportation. Behind the flak gun is a Pz.Kpfw.III. The gun has 7 kill rings painted on the end of the barrel. Barrel rings were usually painted in a contrasting colour – white on a dark grey gun, and black, red, or white on the desert brown and dark yellow used later in the war. Some flak guns saw so much service and scored so many kills that occasionally it was difficult to find room to paint them on the barrel. The majority of flak guns that entered service were primarily used to deal with both aerial and ground threats. As a consequence, hundreds of British and American bombers were brought down, and on the ground the mighty Soviet armoured spearheads were temporarily halted in a number of places.

ABOVE: France, 1944 – a *Luftwaffe* flak crew equipped with a 2cm (0.79in) *Flakvierling* 38 quadrupled-barrelled self-propelled anti-aircraft gun. By 1944, mechanized formations were well equipped with flak guns. There were motorized flak battalions, with divisions being furnished with additional anti-aircraft platoons and companies in the Panzergrenadier, Panzer and artillery regiments. The 'Flak 38' was a formidable weapon able to deal with both low-flying aircraft and ground targets.

ABOVE: The same *Luftwaffe* flak crew as on previous page preparing to go into action with their 2cm (0.79in) quadruple-barrelled self-propelled anti-aircraft 'Flak 38' gun. The crew's commander blows a whistle, signalling to the rest of the men to prepare for action. The gun could release a hurricane of fire, able to discharge 1800 rounds per minute from all four of its barrels. It had a muzzle velocity of 900m/s (2951ft/s) and could engage targets at altitudes of up to 2200m (7220ft). The gun was also very adaptable and could traverse 360 degrees, making it all in-all-a very lethal weapon of war.

LEFT: The *Luftwaffe* flak crew of this 'Flak 38' reload the gun's magazines. By 1944, round-the-clock Allied aerial bombing was causing unprecedented damage. It was not just that factories and homes were being destroyed by the Allied air offensive, thus weakening the German war effort, but also that regular attacks were made against the Panzer divisions. To help stem the serious losses sustained by the air offensive, thousands of flak guns were rushed into service and made widely available to all branches of the armed services, including home defence units.

ABOVE: Russia in autumn 1941. A flak crew manning a 2cm (0.79in) quadruple-barrelled self-propelled anti-aircraft gun. These guns demonstrated outstanding anti-aircraft capabilities. This particular 'Flak 38' gun has been mounted on a river bank in Russia and is probably helping to protect the bridge from enemy attack. Though these weapons were also used on the Eastern Front in an anti-tank role they were not particularly effective against heavy Russian armour.

BELOW: An Sd.Kfz.7 flak halftrack armed with a 3.7cm (1.45in) Flak 36 anti-aircraft gun moves along a road in France in 1940. The vehicle has a full crew on board and the little room afforded them made it difficult to manoeuvre around the gun. On the folding sides of the halftrack additional magazines for the gun could be carried and a single axle trailer stowing more vital equipment and magazines was usually towed. This particular Sd.Kfz.7 probably provided support to one of the Panzer divisions during their advance in France.

RIGHT: Autumn 1941, Russia – a 'Flak 38' is mounted on the back end of an Sd.Kfz.10/4 artillery tractor. The hinged sides and rear railings of the vehicle have been removed to allow extra space on board the halftrack and to provide a wider firing platform for the gunners when the tractor was in action against either aerial or ground targets. The addition of these flak weapons raised the weight of the vehicle by 5.6 tonnes (5.5 tons). Throughout the war, a number of these vehicles were adapted and were seen mounting various guns.

RIGHT: An artillery tractor armed with a 3.7cm (1.46in) Flak 36 gun and shield is supporting ground forces near the river Volga in August 1942. Away from the wide expanses of steppe-land, opportunities for conducting large-scale operations were lost. The war had irretrievably moved on, first into the jagged untamed gullies of the Volga hills and then into the city of Stalingrad, where concrete and stone buildings dominated, making the movement of armoured vehicles almost impossible.

LEFT: Early July 1942, and on the Eastern Front an Sd.Kfz. 10/4 halftrack armed with a 2cm (0.79in) Flak 30 anti-aircraft gun fords a shallow river between Rostov and Voronezh. The vehicle has been embroiled in some heavy contact, judging by the amount of kill markings prominently painted in white on the gun shield. According to this crew, the flak gun has destroyed several armoured vehicles and about eight aircraft. Anti-aircraft defences came into prominence in September 1941, as the Soviet Air force started to inflict heavy casualties.

ABOVE: On the Eastern Front, an Sd.Kfz.7/1 has been equipped with a 3.7cm (1.46in) Flak 36 anti-aircraft gun. The Sd.Kfz 7 weighed 11.2 tonnes (11 tons) and was powered by a 140bhp Maybach water-cooled engine, which provided a top road speed of 50kph (31mph). This vehicle belongs to an unidentified *Waffen-SS* unit in Russia. It was in July 1941 that the *Waffen-SS* received its first medium battery equipped with 3.7cm (1.46in) guns. By 1944, SS mechanized formations were well-equipped with flak guns. The crewmembers are all wearing the M35/40 helmet and *Zeltbahn*.

ABOVE: A flak crew of a 3.7cm (1.46in) Flak 36 anti-aircraft gun mounted on the rear of an artillery tractor in Russia, late summer 1942. The gun's barrel has been elevated towards the sky, the crew having evidently detected enemy aircraft activity. The hinged sides have been completely removed for combat, to allow the crew plenty of space for manoeuvre.

RIGHT: An Sd.Kfz.10/4 halftrack with a 2cm (0.79in) Flak 30/38 anti-aircraft gun guards the approach to a Russian village in September 1941. Of interest is the ammunition trailer attached to the halftrack. The canvas sheeting attached beneath the rear of the vehicle was used to protect the flak gun when it was not in use, and was also used for additional camouflage purposes. As with all halftrack vehicles of this type, the sides of the gun platform could be removed, as in this case, or folded down to provide additional space.

ABOVE: Mounted on the rear of an Opel *Blitz* truck, a 2cm (0.79in) Flak 30 light anti-aircraft gun is being used as a support weapon on the ground against a town in North Africa defended by a group of British soldiers in 1942. The gun weighed 463kg (1020lb) and had a muzzle velocity of 900m/s (2953ft/s). The weapon was very effective and had a fire rate of 120–280 rounds per minute. Throughout the campaign in North Africa the Germans constantly improvised and utilized a number of various commercial vehicles to carry anti-aircraft guns. They were also used against ground targets.

ABOVE: Early August 1941, and a 3.7cm (1.46in) flak gun is mounted on the rear of a 10/4 halftrack near Roslavl-Bryansk. Here, in this swampy and open region, a pocket was hastily formed and German batteries daily brought up greater artillery and flak concentration to bear against a badly depleted Soviet Army. (Red Army strength in the region had initially been estimated to be over 70,000.) The town of Roslavl itself was captured on 3 August, and with it came one of the most swift, as well as one of the most complete, of the German Army's victories in the East.

RIGHT: A *Waffen-SS* anti-tank crew with their 7.5cm (2.95in) PaK 40 somewhere on the Eastern front. The PaK 40 proved its worth in Russia and was more than capable of disabling heavy Soviet tanks. *Waffen-SS* gunners in particular were able to demonstrate their efficacy of the weapon in action in a number of armoured battles in the East. The large splintered shield and low silhouette can clearly be seen in this photograph. The gun weighed 1425kg (3142lb) and could traverse 65 degrees.

ABOVE: A busy *Luftwaffe* flak crew with its 2cm (0.79in) Flak 30 gun in Poland, September 1939. From the amount of discarded ammunition magazines littered around the gun, it is apparent that this Flak 30 has been involved in heavy fighting. This flak gun weighed 463kg (1020lb). It had a rate of fire of 120–280 rounds per minute and had a muzzle velocity of 900m/s (2953ft/s) with a maximum ceiling of 2200m (7221ft). The Flak 30 was the most commonly used light anti-aircraft gun during the Polish campaign and the crews were relatively successful downing what was left of the Polish Air Force.

BELOW: Standing next to his 2cm (0.79in) Flak 38 light anti-aircraft gun, a gunner scours the dawn sky for enemy aircraft in Russia, 1941. Evan at this early stage of the campaign, more than 2000 Soviet aircraft had been destroyed, most on the forward Russian airfield network. Within two days of the attack, more than 500 Red Army bombers had been shot down: the numerically strongest air force in the world had been virtually eliminated in less than 48 hours. The impact of the *Luftwaffe,* supported by its anti-aircraft batteries, forced the Soviets to fight with only minimal air support for the rest of 1941.

ABOVE: A flak crew in action against enemy Russian aircraft in 1942. Judging by the amount of spent bullets on the platform, the gun has seen considerable action. The gun appears to be mounted on either an Sd.Kfz.7/1 halftrack or Sd.Kfz.10/4 halftrack artillery tractor. Although the light anti-aircraft gun was used extensively to deal with the regenerated threat of the Soviet Air Force, the recurring appearance of heavier enemy armour compelled many flak crews to divert their attention from the air and support their own infantry and armour on the ground in an anti-tank role.

RIGHT: An AA machine gunner scans the sky for enemy aircraft. The circular AA sight enables the gunner to calculate the lead he must give to an aircraft flying across his line of fire. Both the modified guns are MG 34 machine guns. The MG 34 was of comparatively lightweight construction and used either drum magazines or 50-round belts. The machine gun had an effective range of 2000m (6565ft) and an impressive rate of fire of 800–900 rounds per minute. This AA MG 34 machine gun could deliver a formidable volume of fire.

ABOVE: June 1941, and on the Eastern Front an AA machine gunner is being transported in a makeshift cart. During these first days of easy victory, the campaign seemed to be running itself. All over the Eastern Front, great prizes beckoned, but already some commanders were concerned that the Panzers were rushing too far ahead. Indeed, horse-drawn transport and soldiers marching on foot were left trailing many miles behind the most advanced armoured spearheads.

ABOVE: Four Sd.Kfz.4/1 *Panzerwerfer 42 Maultier* multi-barrelled rocket launchers on the Eastern Front in winter, 1943. A standard battalion organization had four batteries of six *Panzerwerfer* with a total of 24 launchers. Each rocket weighed 113kg (248.6lb) and had a maximum range of 7850m (25755ft). The *Panzerwerfer* 42 could fire a full salvo in just eight seconds and three full salvoes in five minutes.

BELOW: The crew of a 15cm (5.9in) *Nebelwerfer* 41 on the Eastern Front in 1943 prepare this six-barrelled rocket launcher. The rocket launcher is mounted on the carriage of a slightly modified 3.7cm (1.46in) PaK 35/36. When fully loaded the *Nebelwerfer* 41 weighed 770kg (1694lb) and could fire six 34kg (75lb) rockets to a maximum range of 6900m (22640ft). The soldiers are part of a *Nebeltruppe* (rocket-projector branch).

CHAPTER SIX

Reconnaissance

Gathering Battlefield Intelligence

Probing forward under cover reconnaissance units used a wide variety of armoured cars and motorcycles in order to survey enemy positions. At times in fact, the units that fielded these vehicles were more powerful than the enemy that they would come across.

MOTORCYCLES

Reconnaissance units had what were probably the most dangerous duties to

LEFT: In northern France, two motorcyclists pose for the camera with their motorcycle combination. Motorcyclists were used extensively in 1940 for reconnaissance duties. Their very versatile machines enabled them to survey enemy positions until they encountered enemy fire and then return swiftly with important data and other pieces of vital information relating to the location and strength of the enemy.

undertake on the battlefield. Under cover they had to probe forward, survey enemy positions until they encountered enemy fire and then return with vital information, specifically the location of the enemy. For this reason, reconnaissance units needed a vehicle in which they could retire very quickly. To some extent, the motorcycle suited this task, and each Panzer division had a very capable motorcycle company. In fact, a whole battalion of a Panzer division's rifle brigade were given motorcycles with sidecar combinations. By 1940 BMW and *Zundapp* had mass-produced the motorcycle combinations with very powerful 750cc engines that drove both the rear wheels of the bikes and the sidecar wheels. However, on soft ground or bad roads the motorcycle was quite unsuited, despite its radically

LEFT: An Sd.Kfz.231 *Schwere Panzerspähwagen (6-rad)* passes a line of stationary motorcycles and motorcycle combinations in France, May 1940. Each combination has a tactical number, painted in white on the front of the sidecar. The letter 'G' on the headlamp cover indicates that these vehicles are serving with *General der Panzertruppen* Heinz Guderian. During the French campaign the 1st, 2nd and 10th Panzer Divisions, plus the elite *Großdeutschland* Motorized Infantry Regiment, operated under General Guderian. This photograph was taken just after the 1st and 10th Panzer Divisions had captured the city of Sedan.

improved performance. Although a great number of motorcyclists during the early years of the war rode into battle and dismounted to fight, motorcycles and motorcyclists were regarded as vulnerable to small-arms fire and booby traps. Gradually they were relegated to communication and reconnaissance duties. Nonetheless, motorcyclists on reconnaissance continued to be killed in large numbers. It was therefore decided that the bulk of the reconnaissance forces be given armoured vehicles to protect the crews.

ARMOURED CARS

By 1940 the German Army had more than 600 armoured cars, enough to distribute some 50 or more to each armoured division for reconnaissance duties. Unlike the Allies, the German Army relied heavily on using armoured cars on the battlefield to gain vital intelligence and these were always on hand. Both Army and *Waffen-SS* units were well equipped with armoured vehicles and invariably used a wide range of them in reconnaissance. To ascertain the enemy's strength and intentions, these armoured reconnaissance units were always ready to spearhead an offensive or undertake a daring mission. In combat these armoured cars proved to be potent machines, but sometimes lacked the firepower to fight their way out of danger. It was therefore vital that these vehicles

RIGHT: July 1943, and during Operation Citadel a motorcyclist with an officer as a passenger halts to consult two motorcyclists from an unidentified army *Feldgendarmerie* unit. Both the *Feldgendarmerie* motorcyclists are wearing the silver shield gorget with chain around their necks. The *Feldgendarmerie* was a military body having police powers and forming part of the German Army in the field. It was primarily responsible for traffic control in occupied areas, control duties at ports and airfields, police duties and patrol duties.

maintained their advantages of stealth, speed and surprise if they were to continue gathering intelligence on the battlefield. For this reason a wide variety of armoured cars were fielded as ever more powerful enemy weapons entered service against them.

At the start of the war in September 1939, the German Army and its *Waffen-SS* counterparts possessed a number of various armoured vehicles, which were used primarily in reconnaissance roles. One popular vehicle was the four-wheeled 3.7-tonne (4.1-ton) Sd.Kfz.221. This armoured vehicle was operated by a two-man crew and was armed with a 7.92mm (0.31in) MG 34 machine gun. Another vehicle very popular with reconnaissance units was the Sd.Kfz.222, which was armed with a 2cm (0.79in) KwK 30 cannon and a co-axial 7.92mm (0.31in) MG 34 mounted in an open-topped rotating turret. A rarer variant of this vehicle also used in reconnaissance was the four-wheeled Sd.Kfz.223 radio car. Its main armament was the MG 34 and carried extra communications equipment and an additional third crewmember, who was designated as radio operator. All three of these vehicles were versatile, sturdy machines and could travel extensive distances before refueling. They could also run on the standard German railway gauge with their tyres removed.

Throughout the war the German Army continued to modify a variety of armoured vehicles for reconnaissance. The Sd.Kfz 260 and 261 armoured radio cars were just two of a number of variants that conducted reconnaissance to obtain battlefield intelligence. Both armoured vehicles were open-topped and carried no armament. Under the cover of darkness or hidden in undergrowth or a thick-forested area, these vehicles were solely used for communications work, carrying different configurations of radios and antennae. Another armoured vehicle that helped obtain battlefield intelligence was the

six-wheeled Sd.Kfz.231. This heavy cross-country vehicle was armed with a mounted 2cm (0.79in) KwK 30 cannon in a fully traversing turret, and was manned by a crew of four. A variant of this Sd.Kfz.231 was the Sd.Kfz.232, which carried extra radios and a large overhead aerial frame for signals work.

By 1942 the German Army needed a second generation of tougher armoured cars to carry out reconnaissance duties amidst increased threat from heavy Soviet armour. The result was the production of a heavy eight-wheeled Sd.Kfz.234 armoured car. This vehicle had four variants, the first of which was the basic Sd.Kfz.234/1, which was much heavier than any other previous armoured car. The Sd.Kfz.234/1 was armed with a 2cm (0.79in) cannon. However, a year later in 1943 the vehicle proved to be not powerful enough in combat, and so a more powerful variant was introduced, the Sd.Kfz.234/2 *Puma*. It mounted a powerful long-barrelled 5cm (1.97in) KwK L/60 gun in a revolving turret. Following its debut, the *Puma* soon proved popular within the armoured reconnaissance battalions it served.

The success of the *Puma* led to another variant being built, the Sd.Kfz.234/3. This updated version carried the mighty 7.5cm (2.95in) KwK L/24 gun, which was formerly mounted in pre-1941 Pz.Kpfw.IV tanks. The vehicle was open-topped and consequently ill protected. This led to nervous crews not exposing themselves to hostile fire, preferring almost invariably to remain out of range.

The final version of this variant that entered service in 1944 was the Sd.Kfz.234/4. This vehicle was modified and up-gunned with an even more lethal 7.5cm (2.95in) KwK L/48 gun, which was mounted in an open-topped superstructure. Although it was aimed to be used for reconnaissance missions, its primary role became that of an anti-tank weapon until the end of the war.

BELOW: June 1940, and during the French campaign a motorcyclist is handed what appears to be a radio report from a communications vehicle. The communications trucks invariably stayed close to the front lines, thereby ensuring an uninterrupted radio link between the soldiers fighting on the front lines and units at the rear. Nonetheless, important printed data was sometimes required for dispatch purposes to various sections of the front.

RIGHT: Summer 1942, and two motorcyclists rest in a field. During the early part of the war, a great number of motorcyclists rode into battle and dismounted to fight. They were, however, vulnerable to small arms fire and booby traps, and by late 1941, the motorcyclist was gradually relegated from the front lines to various communication and reconnaissance duties. Even in this new role, casualties remained high. It was therefore deemed necessary as the war progressed that the bulk of the reconnaissance forces be given armoured vehicles to protect the men.

RIGHT: One of the hazards of travelling by motorcycle, especially in the Soviet Union, was the lack of good-quality roads for vehicles. Here, in one of the many forests covering western Russia, a motorcycle dispatch rider watches his comrade repair a punctured tyre. Riding through the great expanses of trees set in tangled undergrowth often proved a perilous undertaking, and the casualty rate among motorcyclists was inevitably high. Fighting in such conditions meant that the Germans were never able to completely clear the woods and that they, therefore, also failed to neutralise the Red Army and partisans. When German patrols accompanied by armour did make a sweep, part of the Russian wood-fighting tactics was to withdraw deeper into the woods until the German patrols passed. Soviet soldiers then re-emerged to engage the follow up infantry, inflicting great casualties upon them in an ambush.

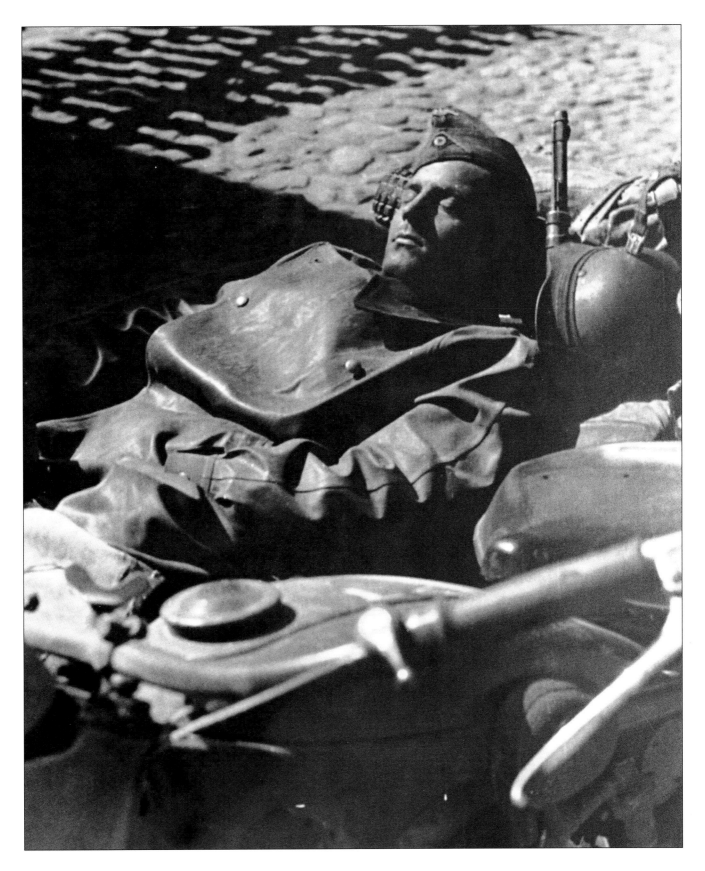

ABOVE: Summer 1942, and a motorcyclist rests inside his motorcycle combination. Travelling by motorcycle across the expanses of the Soviet Union was physically and mentally demanding. The motorcyclist is wearing a double-breasted rubberized motorcycle coat. It was waterproof and was worn with army canvas leather issue gloves or cloth mittens, with overshoes and leggings or army boots. When required equipment was worn over the rubberized motorcycle coat. The rider is wearing the M1938 *Feldmütze*, while his M1935 steel helmet is stowed behind him with his Mauser rifle and kit.

ABOVE: A column of various vehicles, an armoured car and two motorcyclists from the 5th Light Division in Tripoli, 1941. The vehicle at the front is the Volkswagen Type.82.Kfz.1. Its air-cooled engine enabled the car to operate very effectively in the heat of North Africa. The car was quick, agile, tough and able to deal with all types of terrain. It was used not only by the infantry for various supporting roles and reconnaissance, but also by officers. During the course of the war, several variants of the vehicle were manufactured, including a four-seated car; a four-seated survey vehicle; an ambulance, with two seats in tandem on the left side of the vehicle; a three-seated radio car; and even a halftrack version designed to run on railway tracks.

RIGHT: One of the many motorcycle workshops that supported the vast amount of motorcycles deployed on the Eastern Front in 1941. These trainee mechanics make adjustments to their machines under the watchful eye of their instructors. The motorcycle was used for both combat and reconnaissance roles. Each Panzer division incorporated hundreds of motorcycles, distributed among the Panzer and rifle regiments, flak detachments, artillery regiments, Panzer engineers, supply units, Panzer signals and of course the reconnaissance units.

RIGHT: A motorcyclist in his green-grey motorcycle coat. Members of motorcycle units and individual motorcyclists, regardless of rank, were issued with this loose-fitting, rubberized coat. The tail of the coat could be gathered in around the wearer's legs and buttoned in position to allow for easier and safer movement while on the motorcycle. This motorcyclist is also wearing leather gloves, overshoes and leggings. The gas mask canister, when worn in vehicles or on motorcycles, was for comfort's sake normally slung around the neck instead of across the small of the back.

BELOW: Summer 1944, and an officer hitches a lift on the back of a BMW motorcycle as it crosses a pontoon bridge. Hanging beneath the officer is the motorcyclist's leather pannier, which contained the cyclists' personal kit and various maps or paperwork. Leather and canvas were the most commonly used material for motorcycle panniers and kept the items stored inside relatively protected from the elements. A waterproof cape, or *Zeltbahn,* was also stored on the rear of the motorcycle. It gave good protection from the weather while at the same time providing freedom of movement on or off the motorcycle.

ABOVE: A column of armoured vehicles passes through a deserted town near Belgrade during the Balkans campaign in 1941. A rolled-up *Zeltbahn* can be seen on the rear of the sidecar of this motorcycle combination. The size of the rolled up *Zeltbahn* suggests that the motorcyclists have combined a number of *Zeltbahnen* to form a 'pup' tent. The vehicle ahead is an Sd.Kfz.221 armoured car. This four-wheeled armoured car carried a crew of two and was powered by a 75 bhp Auto Union Horch V-8 cylinder petrol engine. It was equipped with a 7.92mm (0.31in) MG 34 machine gun and stowed 2000 rounds.

RIGHT: A motorcyclist pauses to look at his map. He is wearing the standard motorcycle waterproof coat, which has a collar faced in field-grey wool and two large pockets in the front and side, each with a large button-down pocket flap. His gas mask canister is slung on the front of his chest. Of interest are his aviator goggles, which were standard issue to all motorcycle units. Note the torch – this was issued throughout the German Army to all ranks and was designed to be hung from a button on the uniform, fastened by a smaller leather strap fixed to the back of the torch. Motorcyclists were to be found in every unit of a Panzer division, especially during the early years of the war. They were even incorporated in the divisional staff, the brains of the Panzer division, which included a motorcycle messenger platoon. The motorcycle messenger platoon was a vital asset to a Panzer division and enabled the officers and staff to receive and dispatch vital information on the battlefield.

BELOW: 1941, Russia – this motorcycle and combination have been transported inside a motorboat and are now being manhandled out of the vessel with extreme difficulty. A rope tied around the spare wheel is being used to pull the motorcycle combination out of the river. The letter 'B' painted on the rear mudguard of the combination indicates it belongs to Field Marshal Fedor von Bock's Army Group Centre. In June 1941, Bock's Army comprised 42 infantry divisions of the fourth (Kluge) and Ninth (Strauss) Armies and *Panzergruppen II* and *III*. Bock's force contained the largest number of German infantry and Panzer divisions of all three army groups in Russia.

BELOW: In southern Russia, three motorcyclists pause during their journey to relax with a cigarette. They belong to a *Gebirgsjäger* motorcycle unit. Note the *Edelweiss* with white petals, yellow stamens, and a pale green stem and leaves painted on one of the motorcycle's fuel tanks. These

motorcyclists are part of the 1st *Gebirgs*-Division, which was attached to Army Group South. In 1942, the 1st *Gebirgs* Division fought as part of 1st Panzer Army in the Donets area. That summer, it spearheaded the drive into the Caucasus and remained there until 1943.

ABOVE: Fully laden motorcycles and motorcycle combinations follow a convoy of various vehicles consisting of Horch and Opel *Blitz* trucks. The letter 'G' painted in white on the rear of the vehicles indicates that they belong to General Heinz Guderian *Panzergruppe II*. This photograph was taken during the early phases of the Russian campaign, when the weather was very hot and dry and the roads were in relatively good condition. However, German motorized columns could be severely hampered by just a brief downpour of rain, which could easily reduce a dusty uneven road to a slough of mire.

ABOVE: Somewhere in Russia, and a soldier with a map helps two motorcyclists with directions. Moving soldiers from one place to another was an immense logistical problem. Many thousands of maps were produced and distributed to various units at all levels, and this helped reduce the time taken to get from sector to sector. In fact, some maps even showed road states and regulated the daily movement of traffic along the roads within its area.

BELOW: Southern Russia in 1942. Three exhausted soldiers rest next to a motorcycle combination. The motorcycle sidecar can clearly be seen with a crude painting of the *Gebirgsjäger Edelweiss*. The *Gebirgsjäger* were basically light infantry, trained for mountain warfare. The type of terrain where they were operating, dictated the various weapons and equipment they could use. Although motorcycles were used extensively in the *Gebirgsjäger*, units in Army Group South were sometimes obliged to abandon them when leaving the twisting roads of the Caucasus to operate in more mountanous terrian.

LEFT: A mechanic changes the rear wheel of a motorcycle. The 'WH' on the licence plate denotes that it belongs to the *Wehrmacht Heere*, or Army. Except for tanks, halftracks and self-propelled weapons, all German military vehicles were issued with military licence plates. The normal form of an Army licence plate was a white background with a black border and black letters and numbers. The majority of German vehicle license plate numbers were stamped from sheet steel or light alloy. Many plates were held in metal frames, while others were bolted directly to the vehicle's body.

LEFT: **LEFT:** Early October 1941, Russia – a motorcycle and motorcycle combination follow a light Horch car. The letter 'G' painted in white on the rear of the vehicle and on the sidecar of the motorcycle combination denotes that it belongs to General Heinz Guderian's *Panzergruppe II*. These particular vehicles belong to the 4th Panzer Division. It was on 3 October 1941 that the 4th Panzer Division arrived at Orel, following successful attacks from the town of Kromy. This had been a battle of attrition, with serious losses in men and equipment.

ABOVE: Early autumn 1942, and a motorcycle unit negotiates a typical Russian road. The bad road system in Russia severely hindered mobility. This particular road has been severely damaged by the cross-country movement of tracked vehicles. The use of main roads was restricted, generally to priority class vehicles, such as Panzers and halftracks. Next in priority came the ammunition columns and petrol lorry convoys, and then the reinforcements needed to nourish the advance. The nearer to the battle zone, the worse the road system became as vehicles churned up the ground.

ABOVE: Three soldiers struggle to free their motorcycle combination from the mire. For the Panzer divisions on the Eastern Front, mud was a formidable foe. The mud produced from a few hours of rain was enough to immobilize whole columns of wheeled transport, and even tanks. Nor was rain the only problem: the wet season on the Eastern Front began about October, when the first snows came. German commanders observed with alarm how roads vanished in just a few hours and soon realized how dependent they were on the few all-weather roads that had been built in western Russia.

LEFT: Army Group Centre in Russia, October 1941, faces the horrors of mud in the Orel sector. Here, two motorcycle combinations are being towed through the mire. In western Russia, the all-weather roads had not been constructed to carry the amount and weight of traffic that now used them, and the surfaces began to break up under the strain. This road is on the Roslavl highway, here reduced to a mud track nearly a metre deep. In these conditions, horses were often used, but hundreds of them died from heart strain brought on by their efforts to haul the heavy loads of stranded vehicles or artillery pieces through the mud.

ABOVE: Two motorcycle combinations join the exodus of retreating vehicles and horse-drawn transport of the 4th Panzer Division following the defeat at Kursk in July 1943. The division sustained high losses during the battle. After the Soviet counter-offensive was launched on 12 July 1943, the Panzer division engaged in gruelling defensive operations until the end of the year. In June 1944, the division saw more action when the Soviet Army launched Operation 'Bagration'.

RIGHT: A motorcyclist from an unidentified motorcycle unit of the 4th Panzer Division in July 1943. Even by this period of the war, motorcycles were used extensively on the Eastern Front, albeit in communication and dispatch roles only. All the riders were armed with side arms or Mauser rifles slung over their shoulder. Supplies were attached to the back of the bike on panniers. Apart from the rolled-up *Zeltbahn*, they carried the basic kit of an infantry soldier and spares for the motorcycle.

ABOVE: A member of a motorcycle unit passes a stationary Pz.Kpfw.III along a dusty mountain road in the Balkans in April 1941. He is wearing a double-breasted rubberized motorcycle coat, leather gloves, aviation goggles and an Army-issue torch. A Mauser rifle is slung over his shoulder. In the Balkans, the motorcycle was particularly flexible and fast-moving, especially along some of the more open roads.

BELOW: A heavily camouflaged Horch cross-country vehicle, probably on reconnaissance, passes a group of Ukrainian refugees. To ascertain the enemy's strength and intentions, these reconnaissance units were ready to spearhead an offensive or undertake daring missions. Throughout the war, the German Army relied on its armoured reconnaissance units, whose success came from operating stealth and speed.

ABOVE: June 1940, France – a light cross-country Horch Kfz.15 vehicle passes a destroyed house in a French village in June 1940. Heavy foliage has been applied to the vehicle for additional camouflage protection. Of interest are the divisional markings painted in white on the right mudguard of the vehicle. The letter 'K' above the number '17' indicates that it belongs to *Panzergruppe Kleist*. It was General Ewald von Kleist's task to achieve the main breakthrough on the Meuse.

ABOVE: July 1943, and just prior to the battle for Kursk, three crewmembers of a Horch radio car pose for the camera. The number '3' painted in yellow on the door is a sign for the 3rd Company of a signals unit. These vehicles were equipped with a long-range radio set and were most often used by signal units of motorized infantry and Panzer divisions, and also Corps and Army headquarters. The vehicle is still painted in a dark grey base, sprayed over with a camouflage pattern of dark sand.

LEFT: A multitude of armoured cars line a road in eastern Poland in June 1941. These vehicles belong to *Panzergruppe II,* commanded by General Heinz Guderian, and are probably preparing to move into Russia in the rear of the armoured spearheads. The army groups of Guderian and Hoth were to advance as rapidly as possible, forming the jaws of a trap into which the Red Army defending the vast Bialystok salient would fall. The bulk of the German Army was concentrated into two central army groups for two thrusts from Poland. Guderian's *Panzergruppe II,* was directed with its mass of armoured vehicles towards Moscow, whilst the other headed at breakneck speed south east for Kiev, in the heart of the Ukraine.

ABOVE: A group of soldiers belonging to the 2nd SS Panzer Division *Das Reich* pose for the camera next to a heavily camouflaged Volkswagen Type.82.Kfz.1 on 11 July 1943, near Prokhorovka. It was at Prokhorovka on 12 July that one of the greatest tank battle in history between the Germans and Soviets occurred. The battle had severe consequences for the Germans and subsequently halted the armoured advance at Kursk, spelling the end of Operation Citadel.

LEFT: A German sign warns passers-by of an enemy minefield ahead in France, 1940. Two destroyed vehicles can be seen to have already fallen foul of undetected mines. Allied minefields posed a small problem to the German advance in May and June 1940, but the rapidity of the German armoured drive meant that both the French and British were unable to lay extensive mine belts. In fact, so swift were the Panzer divisions that they were able to capture several thousand tonnes of battlefield booty, including huge stocks of mines.

ABOVE: Two captured British P-178 armoured vehicles are on patrol in France, most likely in a reconnaissance role. Unlike the British and French, the Germans relied heavily on battlefield intelligence. The Germans had learnt from the Polish campaign of the need to armour their reconnaissance battalions, and these were now well equipped with armoured cars and halftracks. This weaponry was to also allow armoured reconnaissance battalions to spearhead various offensives.

ABOVE: An Sd.Kfz.263 radio vehicle moves along a road in Tripoli in February 1941. The Sd.Kfz.263 was equipped with a long-range radio set and was used mainly by signal units and Army headquarters. They were protected with canvas covers around the crew compartment and on the telescoping mast antenna. These eight-wheeled, turretless radio armoured cars were used extensively in North Africa. They were particularly useful out in the vast desert with their long-range radio.

ABOVE: A captured British armoured car in North Africa is used as a radio vehicle. All armoured signals vehicles accompanied the advancing Panzers wherever they went, and supplied the communications necessary to let the commanders control their forces effectively. Every command vehicle had a receiving set, and every artillery troop had sets with one principal frequency for emergency use. Radio vehicles were equipped with long-range sets, a vital asset in the middle of the desert.

ABOVE: An Sd.Kfz.263 armoured radio vehicle passes a Horch medium cross-country car in Poland, September 1939. The white cross painted on the engine grill was intended as a distinguishing mark to avoid friendly fire. However, the white crosses became an easy aiming point for Polish anti-tank gunners. Worried crews soon improvised and either painted over the crosses completely or painted out sections of them to make them less conspicuous.

RIGHT: Just two weeks prior to the invasion of Russia, early June 1941, a military ceremony is underway in Germany. An Sd.Kfz.263 radio vehicle is parked on either side of the podium. The Sd.Kfz.263 was equipped with a long radio set and was usually seen in signal units and in Corps and Army headquarters. When these vehicles were out in the field, they were normally protected with canvas covers around the crew's compartment and the telescoping mast antenna. Boxes were hung on the sides to contain stick grenades.

ABOVE: An Sd.Kfz.263 radio vehicle and two Sd.Kfz.221 light armoured cars on parade in Germany, December 1939. The four-wheeled Sd.Kfz.221 armoured car was powered by a 75 bhp Auto Union Horch V-8 cylinder petrol engine. It had a maximum road speed of 80kph (50mph) and a maximum cross-country speed of 32 kph (20mph). The vehicle was equipped with a 7.92mm (0.31in) MG 34 machine gun and proved to be a dependable armoured car, especially in a reconnaissance role. The crews are wearing standard black Panzer uniform and the old Panzer *Schutzmütze* or Panzer beret.

RIGHT: 13 June 1940 between Verdun and the Argonnes – two motorcycle combinations pass a destroyed Sd.Kfz.232 (8-rad) radio vehicle and a four-wheeled Sd.Kfz.221 armoured car from the 8th Panzer Division. It was in this region that fierce fighting erupted against Allied forces determined to hold their positions. But despite strong resistance and the destruction of a number of German armoured vehicles in the area, both the 6th and 8th Panzer Divisions proved too strong and overcame their foe.

ABOVE: Near the Dvina river, a line of armoured vehicles from *Panzergruppe II* drive along a dusty road early July 1941. It was in this area, along the banks of the Dvina, that they met Russian resistance determined to prevent them from gaining a foothold on the opposite bank. Fortunately for Guderian's forces, *Panzergruppe III* had managed to break through further north. This photograph probably shows a reconnaissance patrol just east of the Dvina. Indeed, it was here that reconnaissance proved valuable, enabling *Panzergruppe II* to break through strong Soviet defences and gain a foothold on the far bank on 10 July, a day after beginning the river crossing.

BELOW: An Sd.Kfz.250 halftrack drives along a road in the Balkans in April 1941. Behind it, a StuG.III Ausf.A can be seen with a variety of vehicles in the distance. The Sd.Kfz.250 entered service in early 1940 and first saw combat in May 1940 in the campaign in the West. The standard Sd.Kfz.250 had a combat weight of 5.3 tonnes (5.2 tons) and could reach a top speed of 60kph (37mph). The vehicle featured the same protection as the larger Sd.Kfz.251 halftrack. In France and in the Balkans campaigns, the Sd.Kfz.250 accompanied armour, screening the flanks of the spearheads and carrying troops to the forward edge of the battlefield.

A German unit crosses the Greek frontier on 6 April 1941 during the opening phases of the Balkans campaign. A motorcyclist and an Sd.Kfz.222 four wheeled armoured reconnaissance vehicle are passing through a border point. It was on 6 April that the 12th Army attacked Greece with ten divisions, including two Panzer divisions. Within 24 hours, the Metaxas Line was breached at a number of points, and by 9 April, the 2nd Panzer Division had occupied Salonika and cut off all Greek troops east of the Struma.

ABOVE: 1943, and on the Eastern Front an Sd.Kfz.251 halftrack is about to go into action. At the outbreak of war in 1939, there were some 68 Sd.Kfz.251 halftracks in service. By December 1944, the number peaked at 6146 vehicles. The Sd.Kfz.251 proved a useful supplement to the many truck-borne rifle infantry of Germany's Panzer divisions. At first, the vehicle was not intended to be a combat vehicle, but simply a transporter of infantry to the edge of the battlefield. The Sd.Kfz.251 became so popular within the German Army that there were more than 20 variants constructed during the war.

RIGHT: An Sd.Kfz.251/7 AusfD on the Eastern Front in February 1944 with winter camouflage scheme. Two assault bridge treadways are attached to the side of this pioneer vehicle. This medium personnel carrier was able to carry a crew of twelve. It weighed 7.8 tonnes (7.7 tons) and was powered by a 100 bhp Maybach NL 42 six-cylinder petrol engine. It had a maximum road speed of 52.5kph (32.5mph) and a maximum cross-country speed of 29kph (18mph). This particular halftrack belongs to an unidentified *Waffen-SS* regiment.

ABOVE: Spread out across a field in northern France, a variety of armoured vehicles from the 7th Panzer Division halt while the Luftwaffe soften up enemy defensive positions inside a nearby village. A number of Horch vehicles can be seen, together with a motorcyclist and a halftrack artillery tractor. The artillery tractor with its self-propelled anti-tank gun was a particularly deadly weapon against Allied tanks and armoured vehicles. During the *Blitzkrieg* through France in 1940, heavily armoured reconnaissance vehicles located weak spots in the enemy line and helped maintain the momentum of the attack.

CHAPTER SEVEN

Panzergrenadiers

Motorized Infantry

The Panzergrenadiers were the German motorized infantry and travelled by motor vehicle rather than on foot. The Panzergrenadiers were considered elite frontline units because of their mobility and the fact that they usually found themselves thrust into battle alongside armoured Panzer divisions. With skill and determination, they would advance in trucks and halftracks, which offered armour protection and mobility, until they were close enough to attack enemy positions on foot. The use of motorized infantry was an example of rapid tactical deployment that would change the way battles were fought forever. These troops were always moved into the thick of battle and provided the advancing armour with valuable support. Even during the early part of the war, they conducted mobile operations, invariably accompanying armour, protecting their flanks and being dropped in the middle of a battle to mop up a bewildered and shocked foe.

However, despite its skilful deployment on the battlefield, the grenadier divisions were not removed from the standard infantry formations until later in the war, when they were organized as Panzergrenadiers, or

LEFT: 1940, Belgium – a group of Sd.Kfz.251 halftracks have halted beside a road. The crews watch a small number of French prisoners being marched off to POW camps. For the attack against the West, the offensive was divided into two army groups. Army Group B was given the task of pushing its troops and fast-moving columns through Belgium and Holland. The halftracks carried the infantry into the forefront of the battle.

LEFT: 1942, Russia – two motorcyclists from a Panzergrenadier regiment, both wearing the waterproof motorcycle coat that was a popular and practical item. Motorcyclists were issued with various types of goggles. Kar 98k rifles or MP40 machine guns were the main weapons issued to them. Some motorcyclist combinations, especially those attached to Panzergrenadier regiments, were armed with MG 34 machine guns. An efficient and lethal weapon, the MG 34 was however bulky, whether carried on the lap or attached to the sidecar, and this made it awkward for the soldiers to dismount.

Panzerjäger. It was felt that this new description would boost the morale of the motorized grenadier, who despite the severe lack of vehicles, also fought alongside their tank battalion just like their Panzer division counterparts.

For the remainder of the war the number of elite Panzergrenadier divisions continued to grow and they soon earned the respect of being called the Panzer Elite. With the mounting losses of men and armour, the Panzergrenadier divisions displayed outstanding ability and endurance in the face of overwhelming odds.

HALFTRACKS

The performance of the Panzergrenadiers in battle was attributed mainly to one particular vehicle that transported these infantry units onto the battlefield. It was called the halftrack. These front-wheel steering vehicles with tracked drive transformed the fighting quality of the armoured divisions. They carried the infantry alongside the advancing Panzers and brought machine guns, mortars, boxes of ammunition and supplies, and also towed anti-tank guns and light anti-aircraft guns, howitzers and pontoon-bridge sections to the forefront of the battle. Predominately the main vehicle for carrying infantry and Panzergrenadiers into battle, the halftrack became the preferred vehicle of reconnaissance units as well.

157

ABOVE: A group of infantry move forward into action, supported by a sIG 33 heavy infantry gun, during the Western Campaign in 1940. The infantry usually followed tanks closely to take advantage of their firepower and its paralyzing effect on the enemy's defences. The Panzer or troop-carrying vehicles normally transported the infantry to the edge of the battlefield for speed. The infantry then dismounted at the last moment to charged into action under the protective fire from the tanks. Of interest is the Panzergrenadier going into action armed with an MG 34 machine gun.

Various halftracks were built during the war, including the Sd.Kfz.10 artillery tractor, Sd.Kfz.7/1 self-propelled flak gun, Sd.Kfz.6 and Sd.Kfz.8 prime mover, but the most popular halftrack (and one that was used extensively during the war by the Panzergrenadiers) was the Sd.Kfz.251 medium infantry armoured vehicle. By the time war broke out in 1939, there were only some 68 Sd.Kfz.251 halftracks in service. Although only available in small numbers, the halftrack proved useful even in Poland, transporting infantry to the edge of the battlefield, where they could quickly disembark. Despite being lightly armoured, they could maintain a relatively modest speed and manoeuvre across country and keep up with the fast-moving armoured spearheads.

This advantage (though relatively small) meant that production of the Sd.Kfz.251 steadily increased from 348 during 1940 to some 7800 in 1944, and by the end of the war a staggering 16,000 of them had been built. Throughout the war, as with the bulk of other armour employed for battle, the basic vehicle underwent a series of modifications. In 1939 the first variant, the Ausf.A, entered service. The following year saw the production of the Ausf.B, with a new distinctive shield fitted for the forward MG 34 machine gun. Late in 1940 the Ausf.C made its debut, and finally in 1942, the Ausf.D, the last production model, went into service. This halftrack variant remained unchanged until the end of the war.

It was primarily the success of the Sd.Kfz.251 in France that afforded halftracks a frontline combat role in Russia in 1941. Armed with an MG 34 machine gun, the Sd.Kfz.251/1 was issued to a number of heavy weapons platoons and *Waffen-SS* units. Some Sd.Kfz.251/1 were even modified to fire six 28cm/32cm *Wurfkörper* rockets with lethal effect. Other Sd.Kfz.251 models were also

ABOVE: A group of *Waffen-SS* soldiers from the 4th SS Panzergrenadier Division *Polizei*. A light Horch cross-country car and a motorcycle have halted on a dusty road surrounded by troops. None of the soldiers appear to be armed, suggesting the area has been successfully cleansed of the enemy. By August 1941, the 4th SS Division had been fully committed to battle on the Eastern Front. The *Waffen-SS* grenadiers of the *Polizei* Division were equipped to a lower standard than their counterparts. Used mainly for anti-partisan duties, they often had to make do with obsolete or captured equipment.

159

adapted to carry the standard 8.1cm (3.19in) mortar of a heavy weapons company of a Panzergrenadier battalion. Other variants, like the Sd.Kfz.251/5, were modified with side racks to allow pontoon bridging sections or assault boats to be carried externally. The Sd.Kfz.251/6, although built in limited quantities, was adapted as a command vehicle intended for senior officers.

With its increased combat role, newer variants were given heavier main armaments. In 1941 the Sd.Kfz.251/10 was the first variant to carry a 3.7cm (1.46in) Pak 36 anti-tank gun. Another lethal variant to enter service was the Sd.Kfz.251/9. It was introduced in 1942 and was armed with a very powerful short-barrelled 7.5cm (2.95in) KwK 37 L/24-calibre gun. Other potent halftrack variants continued to make their debut on the battlefield. The Sd.Kfz.251/16 *Flammpanzerwagen* was a mobile flame-thrower that could jet 80 two-second bursts of flame to a distance of 35m (115ft). With the Allied bombing campaign reaching peak levels, the Sd.Kfz.251/17 was introduced. This model mounted a 2cm (0.79in) Flak 30 or Flak 38 on top of the rear compartment. However, by 1944 the losses due to air attack on the *Panzerwaffe* had become so severe that they introduced another variant to try and counter the threat. The Sd.Kfz.251/21 *Flakpanzerwagen* mounted three Luftwaffe 15mm (0.59in) MG 151 machine guns. This was regarded as a relatively cheap but effective conversion and was introduced to anti-aircraft artillery companies of various Panzergrenadier regiments during the last months of the war. The final variant to enter service was the Sd.Kfz.251/22. This model was built in small numbers and carried the 7.5cm (2.95in) Pak 40 anti-tank gun mounted on the fighting compartment of the halftrack. These vehicles were quite successful and considerably enhanced the firepower capability of the Panzergrenadiers.

Another halftrack to see service alongside the Sd.Kfz.251 was the Sd.Kfz.250. This vehicle entered service in 1940 and first saw action during the campaign in France and the Low Countries. As with the Sd.Kfz.251, this halftrack also had a number of variants that were used to fill a variety of roles. The Sd.Kfz.250/1, for instance, was primarily used in armoured reconnaissance and engineering units. Another variant was adapted as a radio vehicle and carried an aerial frame, while the Sd.Kfz.250/7 was a dedicated mortar-carrying vehicle. The next variant, the Sd.Kfz.250/8 entered service in 1943 and was armed with a 7.5cm (2.95in) KwK L/24. Above the main armament an MG 34 was fitted to provide the 7.5cm gun with tracer ammunition so that its crew could get a better sight and range for firing. Yet another variant to see action was the 250/10, which mounted a 3.7cm (1.5in) Pak 36 anti-tank gun. With the ever-increasing need to hold back heavier Soviet armour, more powerful anti-tank guns resulted in the introduction of the Sd.Kfz.250/11 in 1942. This halftrack mounted a powerful 2.8cm (1.1in) *schwere Panzerbüsche 41* taper-bore anti-tank rifle.

Although the number of Sd.Kfz.250 built was only a fraction of the number of Sd.Kfz.251 built, the vehicle was reliable and highly respected by the Panzergrenadiers that used them. Gradually the halftrack that had proven its worth on the battlefield became increasingly vulnerable to enemy fire. During 1944, as the German Army was being harried from both the East and West, the Panzergrenadiers that had supported the armour so valiantly, were now the ones themselves being steadily supported by the dwindling number of Panzers.

LEFT: *Gebirgsjäger* troops mounted on board a Pz.Kpfw.III in southern Russia, 1942. This was the most effective and quick way of reaching the forward edge of the battlefield. The tanks did not have to slow their advance to enable the infantry to keep pace with them. When they arrived at the edge of the battlefield, the tank riders dismounted to let the tank attack and flush out Soviet infantry. When a tank company went into action with infantry, there were normally two platoons on the line, one platoon at the rear, and a fourth in reserve. The interval between tanks was usually 90–110m (300–360ft).

ABOVE: Panzergrenadiers on the Eastern Front in 1941 have dismounted and take cover whilst under fire. Using tanks to take infantry into combat was an effective way of providing additional firepower on the battlefield. The Panzergrenadiers would accompany the armoured spearhead, mounted on board tanks in the first wave, followed immediately by a second wave of Panzergrenadiers in armoured halftracks who would overcome the enemy positions that had survived the first wave.

BELOW: During the invasion of France, infantry advance through a field, closely co-ordinated with armoured vehicles. A PaK 35/36 anti-tank gun is being pushed by a five-man crew. These soldiers are attached to General von Kleist, who commanded units from both the 12th and 16th Armies. *Panzergruppe Kleist* had the critical mission during the French campaign of advancing through the difficult Ardennes and making a rapid crossing of the Meuse.

ABOVE: A group of grenadiers belonging to the 3rd SS Panzer Division *Totenkopf* hitch a lift on board a Pz.Kpfw.III in the Demyansk Pocket in 1942. The tank has received a whitewash coat of paint. A horseshoe has been attached to the tank to bring the crew good luck during their operations in northern Russia. In February 1942 the *Totenkopf* Division had been split into two battle groups and deployed against Red Army forces that were surrounding the Demyansk region. It was in this pocket that the elite band of SS grenadiers were ordered by their beloved *Führer* to stand and fight to the last man.

RIGHT: A group of soldiers prepare to cross the Meuse river on May 1940 with inflatable boats that were used for river assault. One man is inflating his boat with a specially adapted pump. Rope has been attached to the boat so that it can be retrieved swiftly to let more soldiers cross. An Sd.Kfz.251 halftrack has been parked near the riverbank and two infantrymen are attaching a towrope to its the rear. The divisional insignia is painted in white on the rear of the halftrack. The leaf insignia indicates that it is attached to the 1st Panzer Division. It is probable that this photograph was taken along the banks of the Meuse at Sedan.

BELOW: Here, Panzergrenadiers are trying to assist their own vehicle, which is struggling to travel along this muddy road. Bad terrain was a constant problem for wheeled traffic. The appalling mud, coupled with mechanical breakdowns and fierce resistance, caused frequent delays for the infantry, who had to travel long distances on board these vehicles. In some sectors of the front, they were needed desperately, either to replenish depleted units or to be used in a combined arms attack.

ABOVE: Summer 1942, southern Russia – Panzergrenadiers dismount from a StuG.III. The grenadier on the left is armed with an MG 34 machine gun. On the right, his assistant gunner, or *Schütze 2*, is lifting an MG ammunition box. *Schütze 2*'s task was to feed the ammunition belts and ensure that the gun remained operational by clearing jammed rounds or completing various barrel changes. The machine gunner, or *Schütze 1*, was the most experienced and decorated grenadier in the squad and always carried the gun into action. The MG 34, as well as MG 42, were the grenadier's guns of choice during the war.

RIGHT: Spring 1942, Russia – smiling Panzergrenadiers march forward under the protection of a Pz.Kpfw.III. The grenadiers are equipped with Mauser rifles and MP38/40 submachine guns, and many are carrying ammunition boxes. The MP 38 and MP 40 were some of the most successful submachine guns used by grenadiers during World War II, suitable not only for an offensive role, but defensive combat as well. Initially the MP 40 was issued to platoon and section leaders, tank crews, and paratroopers, but it was eventually used throughout the Panzergrenadiers.

BELOW: During Operation Citadel, a group of Russian soldiers surrender to a grenadier. The grenadier is wearing an M1943 steel helmet and *Zeltbahn,* and is armed with an MP 40 submachine gun. The MP 40 weighed 4.7kg (10.4lb), had an effective range of 200m (656ft), and was capable of automatic fire of up to 500 rounds per minute. The first three companies of a Panzergrenadier battalion had a wartime establishment of four heavy and 18 light machine guns, two medium mortars, and 7.5cm (2.95in) guns. The fourth company had three PaK guns. No 9 – the infantry gun company – had six guns mounted on tracks. No 10 Company was the pioneer company, and was equipped with 12 machine guns and 18 flamethrowers.

ABOVE: Two grenadiers investigate a destroyed Russian bunker in 1942. In attacking enemy bunkers or pillboxes, grenadiers used combat groups, which comprised of one platoon of tanks and one platoon of infantry, reinforced by a squad of engineers. Prior to attacking a strong defensive position such as a bunker, artillery was used to weaken the target. Under the protection of this fire, the grenadier units would advance to the bunker with close support of armour.

BELOW: Grenadiers pose for the camera with their Horch cross-country vehicle, which has become bogged down in the relatively soft soil of the Russian steppe. Provisions can be seen, stowed on the rear of the vehicle. Armoured crews and Panzer-grenadiers encountered only minor difficulties on the open steppes of southern Russia. This was regarded as good tank country: there were few roads, but the ground was usually firm enough for both wheeled and tracked vehicles.

RIGHT: September 1942, the Battle of Stalingrad – grenadiers move into action on board an unidentified vehicle. In the distance, the evidence of heavy fighting is apparent, as black smoke rises from a factory burning on the banks of the Volga. The soldier on the right is armed with the 7.92mm (0.31in) Karabiner (Kar) 98b carbine bolt-action rifle, the most common weapon in the grenadier's arsenal. It weighed 4kg (8.8lb) and had a maximum magazine capacity of five rounds. Both grenadiers are wearing the regulation Army-issue camouflage helmet cover.

BELOW: During a short lull at Stalingrad, a group of grenadiers rest under the protective cover of an Sd.Kfz.251 command vehicle. The troops are all wearing the German Army M1936 service uniform, which was worn in the field under combat conditions. The soldiers are well equipped with Kar 98K pouches, bread bag, entrenching tool, cape bag, personal kit and water bottle. Three of the soldiers are wearing 6 x 30 binoculars around their neck.

RIGHT: Various halftracks and personnel carriers are spread out across a field in France in 1940 to make a more difficult target for enemy bombing or artillery fire. A number of Sd.Kfz.251 and Sd.Kfz.10 halftracks can clearly be seen. In the foreground, the crew of an Sd.Kfz.10 are partially hidden by an unfolded *Zeltbahn*. The *Zeltbahn* not only protected the troops from the rain and cold, but also afforded some camouflage protection. At this period of the war though the *Luftwaffe* still had total supremacy of the air, hence most units did not scatter their vehicles in this way.

BELOW: Trucks laden with infantry cross a pontoon bridge in France in 1940. The infantry of the German Army considered itself to be the most important component of the armed services. It contained the greatest number of men, and its combat ability had been the means of Germany's triumph in Poland. Only the infantryman was able to defeat the enemy on the field of battle and go on to hold the ground that had been won. The infantry soon found that, when in support of armour, it could contest even greater firepower and achieve more ground more quickly, with lower casualties. Out of the infantry regiments were born the Panzergrenadiers, who travelled mainly by motor vehicles rather than on foot.

ABOVE: An Sd.Kfz.251 *Kommandopanzerwagen* makes its way along a muddy road. These specialized vehicles were intended for senior commanders and were produced in limited quantities. The Sd.Kfz.251 was the most popular vehicle used by the Panzergrenadiers and was frequently seen in the thick of battle, moving alongside tanks and providing the latter with valuable support. However, it was not until Russia, when the grenadiers were given a greater combat role, that the halftracks were equipped with heavier main armament to give it even greater offensive punch.

169

ABOVE: Preparing to go into the thick of battle in their Sd.Kfz.251/9, a *Waffen-SS* soldier cleans the barrel of a 7.5cm (2.95in) KwK 37 L/24-calibre gun. The *Waffen-SS* acquired its first Sd.Kfz.251 halftracks only in 1942, when Hitler decided to upgrade the *Das Reich, Leibstandarte* and *Totenkopf* divisions for the war in the East. An Sd.Kfz.251 carried a 10-man *Waffen-SS* rifle squad plus their MG 34 machine gun. These halftracks were often seen in the thick of battle, debussing their troops and mopping up the enemy before returning to be moved to another battle line.

RIGHT: An Sd.Kfz.251 command vehicle halts and an officer give out orders to the commander of a Panzergrenadier unit in 1943. By this period of the war the the Sd.Kfz.251 had become not just a halftrack intended to simply transport infantry to the edge of the battlefield, but also a fully-fledged fighting vehicle. It had a good cross-country performance and could keep up with fast-moving Panzer forces. Because of its speed, Panzergrenadiers extensively used the Sd.Kfz.251 throughout the war where the vehicle could also provide valuable fire support in the thick of battle.

ABOVE: A column of StuG.III.Ausf.G laden with infantry in Poland in October 1944. To maintain their speed, the accompanying infantry were carried into battle on the tanks and other armoured vehicles. When they ran into stiff opposition, they immediately dismounted to avoid taking heavy casualties.

These late-variant StuG.III assault guns still retain their summer camouflage scheme of brown patches over the dark sand base. All three armoured vehicles have a thick coating of *Zimmerit* anti-magnetic mine paste. The middle StuG is missing *Schürzen* plates indicating that it has been embroiled in heavy combat.

ABOVE: An Sd.Kfz.251 and an Sd.Kfz.10 advance through a French village in 1940. Painted on the rear of the Sd.Kfz.251 is the divisional tactical insignia that indicates it is attached to the 1st Panzer Division. During the invasion of France, the Sd.Kfz.251 proved a useful supplement to the predominantly truck-borne rifle infantry of the Panzer divisions. It was relatively lightly armoured in order to maintain speed across country and to keep up with the fast-moving Panzer units.

BELOW: A column of Sd.Kfz.251 halftracks ford a river in Russia in 1941. By this period of the war, halftracks were given a frontline combat role, which increased the vulnerability of both the Panzergrenadiers it carried and the vehicle itself. However, during the summer of 1941, Sd.Kfz.251 halftracks achieved remarkable success and held their own in the thick of battle. Time after time, they screened the flanks of the spearheads and debussed their grenadiers in the midst of battle.

LEFT: A group of Sd.Kfz.251 halftracks attached to *Panzergruppe Kleist* on the Eastern Front in 1941. These grenadiers have moved into a nearby village and mopped up a handful of Russian prisoners. A Russian soldier stands in front of a halftrack and handful of POWs can be seen in the halftrack behind the Russian soldier. By 1942, transporting Red Army prisoners by armoured vehicle had become increasingly rare, and by the later stages of the war, the German Army followed a shoot to kill policy of all captured Russian soldiers.

ABOVE: During the initial stages of the Russian campaign in July 1941, a ferry has transported armour from the Sixth Army to the banks of a river. An Sd.Kfz.7 halftrack has just driven off the ferry and has halted next to a Pz.Kpfw.II. Even by the end of 1941, the German armoured force still seemed invincible. However, a few months later, when the Sixth Army was ordered to press southeast towards Stalingrad on the Volga River, it lost its advantages of mobility and firepower, and became irreversibly embroiled in terrifying street fighting. The capture of Stalingrad was an important objective, to give the German Army access to Astrakhan and the vital supply of petroleum from the south.

BELOW: A group of British soldiers captured by the 8th Panzer Regiment near the Halfaya Pass in North Africa in June 1941. They are being transported to the rear inside an Sd.Kfz.251 halftrack. The Sd.Kfz.251 was a revolutionary design for armoured vehicles that carried troops into battle: it had rear doors and the crew compartment was left open so that infantry could quickly disembark over the sides. The superstructure was protected by 1.45cm (0.6in) of armour plate on the front and 0.8cm (0.32in) on the side and rear. The halftrack was widely used in the *Afrika* Korps.

LEFT: May 1941, Tobruk – a Sd.Kfz.251 and its crew moves through the North African desert. An MG 34 machine gun is mounted on the top of the halftrack, which has been covered with canvas to protect it against the desert sand. The vehicle carries a hood, not only to protect the 10-man crew from inside, but also to afford some camouflage protection in the open desert. The divisional command pennant denotes the presence of an officer. When the officer was not in the halftrack, the pennants were either removed or covered.

ABOVE: Troops from the 5th Panzer Regiment have come to a halt south of Tobruk in June 1941. On the left stands a Pz.Kpfw.III Ausf.F. On the right is an Sd.Kfz.251 with nearly a full compliment of men on board. Here, in the open desert of North Africa, the halftrack continued to support the armoured spearhead. The huge expanses of open terrain were relatively good tank country: halftracks laden with well-armed troops were able to keep in close formation with other vehicles.

RIGHT: July 1943, the Kursk bulge – grenadiers move into action through a ploughed field in close support of a StuG.III. Ausf.G assault gun. A few of the grenadiers have managed to hitch a lift on board the assault vehicle. Carrying full kit, they are equipped with the Kar 98K rifle. Note the soldier in the foreground with fixed bayonet. During the Battle of Kursk, the combined strength of both the 9th Army and 4th Panzer Army was roughly 700,000 men, 2000 tanks and assault guns, and 1800 aircraft.

ABOVE: During this summer of battles in 1942, troops from an unidentified *Gebirgs*-Division of Army Group South pass one of many abandoned Soviet bunkers. These mountain troops are not fighting in their natural element and had little opportunity to demonstrate their skills as alpine soldiers. However, in conventional battle, across the flat and arid wilderness of the Soviet Union, they often excelled against heavy Russian fire, especially when supported by armour. By the late stages of the war, these superbly trained soldiers often found themselves thrown into the line as ordinary infantry.

BELOW: During Operation Citadel, a *Waffen-SS* grenadier unit advances through a sunflower field. This clearly illustrates the effectiveness of their camouflage smocks and helmet covers. The grenadier nearest the camera and without a camouflaged helmet cover is wearing an early style 'Plane Tree' pattern camouflage smock. His personal equipment is unusually limited to his belt and P-38 holster. The other two grenadiers appear to have a full set of combat equipment, including magazine pouches, entrenching tool, aluminium water bottle, mess tin, bread bag, and gas mask canister.

BELOW: Late autumn 1944, the Eastern Front – the commander of a crowded Sd.Kfz.251/3 Ausf.C command halftrack relays orders to the commander of an Pz.Kpfw.IV Ausf.J. The grenadier approaching the cameraman is armed with an MP 40 submachine gun. By 1944, armoured units suffered increasing numbers of enemy air attacks as the *Luftwaffe* lost control of the skies. In an attempt to curb the losses, most crews camouflaged their vehicles with foliage, as can be seen with this halftrack. Interestingly, the crew of the Panzer have made no attempt to conceal their vehicle from the air.

LEFT: On the Eastern Front, troops from *Kampfgruppe 'Nord'* (later known as the 6th SS-*Gebirgs*-Division 'Nord') support an armoured spearhead towards Murmansk. These *Waffen-SS* troops are wearing two-piece snowsuits and are armed with Kar 98K rifles, and appear to be collecting snow for drinking water. These troops were one of the first units to see action in the far north sector of the Eastern Front. In this frozen cold and dark forest, which covered many hundreds of square miles, *Kampfgruppe 'Nord'* suffered heavy casualties at the hands of very strong Soviet resistance.

ABOVE: Late 1941, soldiers attached to *Kampfgruppe 'Nord'* take cover in the snow from heavy Soviet fire. The photographer has also taken evasive cover: crouching beside the wheels of a Pz.Kpfw.III, he is photographing a soldier who lies face down in the snow, presumably fatally wounded. In the distance, a group of *Gebirgsjäger* ski troops are taking cover behind some trees. All the troops are wearing heavy padded reversible clothing. The jacket has an integral hood, and access to the uniform underneath via the pockets. The steel helmets have all been whitewashed to give additional camouflage protection.

RIGHT: A *Waffen-SS Ski-Jäger* Brigade moves through the snow under the protection of a group of Pz.Kpfw.IIIs. The ski-trooper wears the standard grey-to-white anorak. Although these snow suits provided good camouflage, they soon became dirty, thus defeating the object of the white camouflage. Soldiers were therefore supplied with a thin white cotton cover or cape, which could be worn over the uniform and equipment, and could easily be washed and cleaned.

ABOVE: A group of officers attached to the *Gebirgs-Panzerjäger Abteilung 157* of the 6th *SS-Gebirgs*-Division 'Nord' have hitched a lift on board a Pz.Bef.Wg.III. Ausf.H. Two of the officers wear camouflage suits. The office who holds a pair of 6 x 4 binoculars sports a stitched black armband. The armband was designed to distinguish between friend or foe in the snowy terrain where the enemy wore white as well. He is also wearing a whitewashed steel helmet and heavily padded mittens.

LEFT: Late 1943, and an officer attached to *SS-Panzerjäger Abteilung 6* is seated inside an armoured vehicle. To his right, a soldier in a white camouflage suit is holding a whitewashed Mauser rifle. This photograph was taken when the newly formed 6th *SS-Gebirgs*-Division 'Nord' was serving in the Finnish Karelia sector. By December 1944 the division had been transported to Belgium.

BELOW: Officers and soldiers attached to the *Gebirgs-Panzerjäger Abteilung 157* of the 6th *SS-Gebirgs*-Division survey the terrain for the next strategic movement. The 6th Gebirgs-Division took part in the main drive into Russia, towards the port of Murmansk. It remained in the far northern sector of the Eastern Front until late 1944, when Finland surrendered to the Russians.

BELOW: Late 1943, and ski troops from *SS-Panzerjäger Abteilung 6*, which was attached to the 6th SS *Gebirgs*-Division 'Nord', advance through the snow. They are supported by Pz.Kpfw.IIIs, which provided the troops the added punch for an attack. Both *Wehrmacht* and *Waffen-SS Gebirgsjäger* soldiers were adequately armed and equipped, but had little opportunity to demonstrate their unique, alpine skills. They fought with skill and tenacity, but their expertise wasted, for they were employed as assault infantry in conventional battle, for which they had little training.

LEFT: Summer 1942, southern Russia – *Gebirgsjäger* troops advance through thick smoke following vicious fighting. The *Gebirgsjäger* fought in both extremes on the Eastern Front, and their operations in the Caucasus almost took them out of Europe and into Asia. Indeed, during World War II, there was no campaign in which the mountain troops did not fight. To overcome the problems associated with warfare in alpine terrain, the *Gebirgs* divisions were equipped with weapons and transport quite different from those found in standard infantry divisions.

LEFT: A grenadier armed with a flamethrower ignites a lethal burst of burning fuel across some barren terrain. The flamethrower remained a rare weapon during World War II, but was nonetheless valuable to both the *Wehrmacht* and *Waffen-SS* grenadiers. However, the weapon had a limited range and the grenadiers found it bulky and cumbersome to carry. Having to hold in one hand the projector and the fuel tank that was attached to the back, users complained of having difficulty mounting and debussing from armoured or halftrack vehicles.

ABOVE: *Waffen-SS* Panzergrenadiers have halted in a town in East Prussia in early January 1945. Three Sd.Kfz.251 halftracks laden with troops are parked on the road. By this period of the war, SS Panzergrenadiers were not so much supporting the tanks as being supported by them. Day by day, in this period known as 'Black January', the Panzergrenadiers fought to the death as East Prussia quaked under the tread of Russian armour. The Soviet front stretched some 480km (300 miles) across Prussian territory into the Baltic States: the whole of the Reich would soon be overrun.

ABOVE: During Operation Blue in May 1942 grenadiers march into a deserted village. The grenadier at the end of the column has an MG 34 machine gun slung over his left shoulder. This was the world's first general-purpose machine gun, and was used by grenadiers in both a light and heavy role. Weighing only 11.5kg (25.4lb), it was more portable than its predecessors. The machine gun possessed a wooden shoulder stock, pistol grip and a V-notch rear sight. This solid construction stood the test of combat and the harsh weather conditions that the grenadiers encountered.

ABOVE: A group of grenadiers armed with 98K Kar rifles push forward during the summer of 1942 across the seemingly endless Russian landscape. Panzergrenadiers were regularly seen scouting ahead of armour. On most occasions, they were deployed on the flanks to guard against enemy counterattacks as the German armour smashed through enemy defensive positions. When the Panzers had successfully captured a position, halftracks and other infantry-carrying vehicles moved back in to collect the grenadiers.

BELOW: Summer 1943, Russia – troops have a chance to rest after a successful armoured breakthrough. Various vehicles, including Horch cross-country cars, are spread across the Russian steppe. Out on the vast open landscape, grenadiers were constantly vulnerable to enemy fire and, as a consequence, they increasingly abandoned their flank protection role. Instead, they took the primary responsibility for locating and neutralizing enemy anti-tank gun nests and dispersing enemy infantry tank-hunting units.

LEFT: Out on the Russian steppe, soldiers stop to collect water during a lull in the fighting in 1942. The steppe was notorious for its lack of drinking water, and many veterans from this area vividly recall their constant thirst, especially during the hot summer periods. Nonetheless, the landscape did have its advantage as both armoured crews and grenadiers regarded it as good tank country. Although there were few roads, the ground was often firm enough in dry weather for it to be used by wheeled or tracked vehicles.

ABOVE: Taken in 1942, this photograph shows a line of halted Sd.Kfz.251 halftracks. The vehicle name, 'Nikolajew', is painted in white on the side of the halftrack. The practice of naming individual vehicles was not widespread in the German Army. When vehicles did carry names, these were often chosen for reasons of identification as much as morale. Some vehicles took their name from a city, province or region in Germany, while a very few were named to celebrate the capture of an important city or town. The name on this vehicle is probably named after the southern Russian city of Nikolayev, near the Black Sea.

ABOVE: February 1943, Kharkov – elite Panzergrenadiers, from the 2nd SS Panzer Division *Das Reich,* on board a tank. It was just northwest of the city of Kharkov that Soviet forces were temporarily stalled by units of the *Das Reich* division. Hitler had ordered the SS to retake the city at all costs – and then hold it.

On 12 March 1943, units of the *Das Reich* entered the city and reached the main railway line. After linking up with elements of the 1st SS Panzer Division *Leibstandarte SS Adolf Hitler,* they smashed into the east and southeastern sectors of the city to flush out what remained of the Russian forces trapped inside.

RIGHT: The Battle of Kursk in 1943. Pictured are Panzergrenadiers from the 2nd SS Panzer Division *Das Reich.* Nearly one million German soldiers tried to smash their way through six Soviet defensive belts, the attack soon becoming a battle of attrition. In this photograph, the grenadiers observe the devastation of the battlefield from a captured trench. A number of Soviet T-34s can be seen knocked out, probably following a vicious clash of arms during the early stages of the attack.

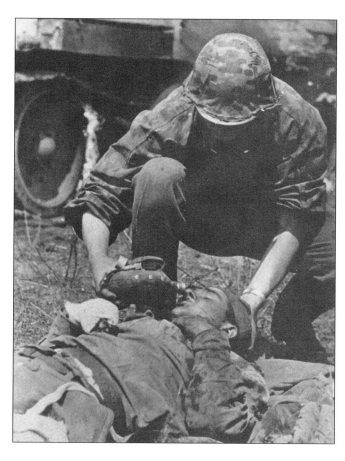

LEFT: This photograph was probably taken during Operation Citadel. The remains of a Soviet T-34/76 Model 1943 blaze in the background, while a *Waffen-SS* grenadier gives a wounded tank man a drink of water from his M1931 field flask. Soviet losses during the battle were significant and, according to Soviet reports, more than 177,847 troops out of a total committed strength of 1,272,700 personnel were killed or injured. Despite these losses, the Soviet mobile force had fought the Germans to a standstill, but the cost was high: a delay in the capture of Kharkov and a loss rate of tanks almost eight times that of the Germans.

BELOW: After debussing from a *Kubelwagen* type166.Kfz.1/20 light cross-country amphibious *Schwimmwagen,* two *Waffen-SS* grenadiers machine-gunners rush to take cover. The machine-gunner is equipped with a 7.92mm (0.31in) MG 42. The MG 42 was the finest machine gun of World War II. It had excellent handling qualities and was extensively used by *Waffen-SS* grenadiers, having tremendous capabilities in battle and able to fire up to 1550 rounds per minute. As with the MG 34, its individual belts could be clipped together for more sustained fire. In effect, a typical nine-man grenadier squad existed to service the machine gun, and just a couple of these well sighted and well supplied MG 42 guns could hold up an entire attacking regiment for hours. Here, the grenadier clutching two MG ammunition boxes is the assistant gunner, or *Schütze 2.*

RIGHT: During Operation Citadel, an SS grenadier armed with an MP 40 stands guard over a captured Russian infantryman, who is tending to a wounded comrade. Behind them, a knocked out Russian T-34 tank blazes. The grenadier is wearing a 'Plane Tree' pattern camouflage helmet and an early-style 'Palm' pattern camouflage smock, which was originally introduced in 1940. The Kursk strategic operation proved very costly to both sides, but the Soviets, with their massive Red Army, could afford the losses while the Germans most definitely could not. The Soviets now had the initiative and exploited their victory to the full: there were to be no more periods of quiet on the Eastern Front.

BELOW: Another photograph depicting a scene from Operation Citadel. An MG *Waffen-SS* grenadier squad rests inside an armoured vehicle following a brief lull in the fighting. The *Schütze* 1, or machine gunner, rests his head on the wooden shoulder stock of the fully loaded MG 42 machine gun. The weapon has been attached to a tripod mounting, which could be quickly released and carried into action by hand. The other two members inside the armoured vehicle are probably other members of the squad, who brought up fresh ammunition for the gun. A typical MG 42 squad consisted of a gunner, loader, and a munitions carrier.

ABOVE: Operation Citadel again, and an MG *Waffen-SS* grenadier squad hitches a lift on board a tank. The soldier on the left is armed with an MG 42 machine-gun; to his left, his comrade is armed with an MP 40 sub-machine gun. When the squad debussed to go into action, the majority of the squad generally deployed themselves in foxholes to cover all possible approaches to the newly set-up machine-gun nest. Although squads did sustain high losses in this way, they could remain very effective, protecting the flanks and keeping open a path for the armour to pour through.

ABOVE: A fully equipped group of grenadiers prepare to move forward into action. The MG 34 machine-gunner and assistant gunner have both added foliage and grass to their steel helmets. This method of camouflage was used to varying degrees, but all had the desired effect of breaking up the helmet's sharp outline. It also helped, to some extent, to make the helmet surface non-reflective. The soldiers pictured here have blended in quite well with the local surroundings.

LEFT: During the Western campaign in 1940, a soldier manning a field telephone keeps low in a field. He is probably in a forward observation post, collating important information for various units following up from the rear. Panzer-grenadiers constantly probed enemy positions, relaying messages to other advancing units and instructing them on the various dispositions of their opponents. By undertaking such a risky task, grenadiers were able to keep open the flanks and allow the armour to move forward relatively unmolested.

ABOVE: Operation Citadel and during its initial stages an *Waffen-SS* grenadier is equipped with a fully loaded MG 42 machine gun. A destroyed T-34 tank and a burnt-out Russian truck is evidence of heavy combat in the area. On the battlefield, *Waffen-SS* grenadiers sought to deploy their machine guns in the most advantageous defensive positions, and employed elaborate camouflage to protect them. This MG grenadier has clearly taken up a temporary position; when time and conditions allow, he will simply pick up his machine gun and move forward to another position.

BELOW: Summer 1943, the Ukraine – Panzergrenadiers advance through a field under the protection of an Sd.Kfz.251 halftrack. Captured Russian prisoners can be seen, flanked by the grenadiers. By this period of the war, the Soviet Army in the Ukraine and Belorussia was gathering momentum. By August, Kharkov was retaken; the following month, the Red Army recaptured Smolensk and Bryansk. In October, the German Army suffered another blow, as the Kuban bridgehead opposite the Crimea was destroyed, closing the route to the Sea of Azov to German shipping. By 6 November 1943, the Ukrainian capital of Kiev was retaken by the Soviets.

RIGHT: Spread out across the Russian steppe, a variety of armoured vehicles present a smaller target in case of bombing or heavy artillery fire. The crew of an Sd.Kfz.251 nap on top of the engine deck of the vehicle. Draped over the rear part of the fighting compartment is a national flag, used for aerial recognition. The remainder of the halftrack's fighting compartment has been covered by a *Zeltbahn,* which also conceals the vehicle's MG 34 machine gun and shield. It is more than likely that other grenadiers are sleeping beneath the *Zeltbahn.* The old style *Balkenkreuz* on the side of the halftrack is painted in black with a white outline.

BELOW: A rare glimpse at *Waffen-SS* Panzergrenadiers in the thick of battle during the early stages of Operation Citadel. Here, grenadiers go into action against Red Army targets. Their main task was to spearhead the attack, clearing the ground of enemy infantry and anti-tank guns and allowing the armour to pour through unhindered. The success of any grenadier during the thick of battle depended squarely on quick reactions and daredevil tactics. Not surprisingly, many troops, particularly those attached to the *Waffen-SS,* were killed. But in spite of paying a heavy price for every metre captured, the grenadiers carried on, moving from one dangerous spot to another, and penetrating enemy positions.

ABOVE: An Sd.Kfz.251 complete with antennae trundles along a road on the Eastern Front in the summer of 1943. The Sd.Kfz.251 was a very robust and reliable vehicle, and was used extensively to transport grenadiers into battle. Once the area had been cleared, the grenadiers would board the vehicle once more and be taken to another dangerous spot, where they would debus and begin the process all over again.

BELOW: A StuG.III has halted on a road next to a Sd.Kfz.251 during the initial stages of the Soviet summer offensive code-named operation 'Bagration' in 1944. By this stage of the war Panzergrenadiers were extensively transported by halftracks into battle. The vehicle's 100 bhp Maybach NL 42 six-cylinder petrol engine had a maximum road speed of 52.5kph (32.5mph) and 29kph (18mph) cross-country.

ABOVE: Two Sd.Kfz.251 halftracks laden with Panzergrenadiers move through a forest during the early autumn of 1941. These soldiers were part of Guderian's Panzergruppe II. These men would soon become embroiled in heavy fighting west of

Moscow. However the winter, coupled with determined Russian resistance prevented Guderian's armoured might from reaching the Soviet capital. Even with the support of the Panzer-grenadiers, further attempts to move forward proved futile.

RIGHT: *Waffen-SS* grenadiers move across the battle zone following a series of successful deep penetrations against a number of enemy defences during the summer of 1943. Two Pz.Kpfw.IVs can be seen in the background supporting the attack. By 1945 Panzergrenadiers were fighting in small mobile groups with tanks. Although the Panzergrenadiers' days were numbered by early April 1945, they continued to fight on from one desperate battle zone to another.

CHAPTER EIGHT

Support Vehicles

Vital Modes of Transport

Preparing for action relied on various light and heavy trucks and many civilian and armoured vehicles for transport. Maintaining the momentum of an armoured advance was vital to success, and without support vehicles, the whole advance might stall.

COMMERCIAL VEHICLES

By 1939 there was a wide variety of commercial vehicles in Army service: cars, motorcycles, light and heavy cross-country and transport trucks. These support vehicles were a necessity for any armoured force preparing to go into action, allowing it to function in a cohesive and well-defined manner. The support vehicles also made a vital contribution to the Army's drive forward, especially when leading units were far ahead of its column. Transport vehicles too, including haulage trailers and tractors, were an important component, vital for towing or carrying bridging equipment, hauling the many millions of spare parts for the massive array of tanks, armoured cars, halftracks and other support vehicles. These support vehicles were constantly needed, especially for tracked vehicles. Even in unopposed movement, there was extreme wear and tear to these machines. What's more, tank tracks themselves could inflict terrible damage upon the road surface, and this often caused considerable problems for transport following behind the Panzers,

LEFT: Troops in France in 1940 unload parts of a bridging section from the rear of a lorry. A typical Panzer division consisted of a multitude of support vehicles, including engineering trucks, radio vehicles, personnel carriers, Horch trucks, Opel *Blitz* A-type kitchen lorries, fuel tankers, Büssing Nag 500 A and Henschel 33GI troop carriers, haulage trucks and tractors. A number of civilian lorries were also used. These vehicles were flimsy by German military standards and a far cry from the preferable Krupp trucks.

LEFT: Early spring 1942, and on the Eastern Front a group of soldiers try desperately to push their Opel *Blitz* truck through the mire. Such struggles were a common sight. Support vehicles, though a necessity, were given low priority on the road dispatcher's list.

since few trucks had four-wheel drive. The Panzer itself was not a very reliable machine and needed frequent repairs. Each division was subsequently given three mobile workshops, two with 10.9-tonne (12-ton) repair vehicles and one with 21.8-tonne (24 ton) repair vehicles.

A typical Panzer division in 1940 consisted of literally dozens of various light and heavy support vehicles. The Büssing Nag 500 A, Krupp-Protz Kfz 81, 3-Ton Ford Type G917T, 3-Ton Ford Type 3000, Henschel 33GI, Opel *Blitz* Bus, Opel S-type fuel tanker Kfz 385, Opel *Blitz* A-type kitchen, Personnel carrier Kfz 70, Horch 830 B, Tatra 57 K, Mercedes-Benz 320 Model 1939, Mercedes-Benz L 1500 A, Austrain Steyr 640, Austrian 1500 A Series, Engineering truck on chassis Kfz 61, Ambulance 25H Kfz 31 and the Skoda H 65T6-T, were just some of the vehicles that supported a Panzer division's advance through France.

Divisional transport amounted to some 452 motorcycles and 942 light and 1133 heavy lorries. Each division also relied on hundreds of horses to tow guns and carts. This in itself demanded much manpower and resources, and horse-drawn transport had trouble supplying motorized and tank units during the Polish campaign. The experience there demonstrated how dangerous things could become when support vehicles failed in supplying the most forward elements of an armoured division. Maintaining the momentum of an attack was vital to success, and without vital provisions – including spare parts, fuel, ammunition and food stocks – the whole advance was jeopardized. Despite such huge logistical problems, the support vehicles were relatively successful at maintaining momentum. Serious trouble occurred only when the road system was poor.

ARMOURED SUPPORT VEHICLES

Apart from the various light and heavy trucks and the many civilian vehicles that were used by the Army to supply the main divisional advance, there were a number of armoured vehicles that closely supported the armoured spearheads. One particular vehicle was the Volkswagen Type.82.Kfz.1. This light field cross-country personnel carrier was popularly known to the soldiers that drove it as the *Kubelwagen*, *Kubelsitzer*, or simply *Kubel*, all derived from *Kubelsitzwagen*, or 'bucket-seat car'. The Type.82 *Kubelwagen* was mass-produced, some 55,000 of them seeing extensive service during World War II. Its air-cooled engine enabled the car to operate effectively in both the heat of North Africa and the freezing conditions of the Eastern Front. Quick, agile, tough and able to deal with all types of terrain, the *Kubelwagen* proved to be a truly remarkable and very reliable independent machine that was used not only by the infantry, but officers as well. During the course of the war, variants of the *Kubelwagen* were produced, including a four-seated car; a four-seated survey vehicle; an ambulance, with two seats in tandem on the left side of the vehicle; a three-seated radio car; and even a halftrack version designed to run on railway tracks.

One of the most popular variants of the *Kubelwagen* was the 166.Kfz.1/20 light, cross-country, amphibious *Schwimmwagen*. The vehicle was a four-wheel drive and had a boat-like body with full-length fenders. Propulsion in water was provided by a three-bladed propeller geared to the engine and mounted on a hinged arm. The vehicle could reach a maximum speed of 6 knots in the water and 80kph (50mph) on land. Some 14,265 *Schwimmwagens* were produced between 1942 and 1944. Some of them received additional armour plating to protect the occupants from small arms fire. Other vehicles also provided close support for the main divisional drive. These also included civilian vehicles such as the BMW 326 two-door convertible and the Wanderer W 50 and Renault AHN 3-ton truck. The Horch cross-country car, Opel *Blitz* S-type 3 ton truck and the Steyr Type.1500 A, were also regularly seen on the front lines. Due to the increasing threat of air attack, a majority of these vehicles received bold camouflage patterns. During late 1942 a new type of vehicle started to appear in the Panzer divisions: a semi-tracked transport truck designed for multi-purpose service on the Eastern Front. The truck was specially designed to overcome the appalling road surfaces that constantly plagued the support vehicles' advance. But despite the various modifications and the drastic attempts to conceal them from enemy attack, the support vehicles were losing more than could be replaced. Even captured trucks and motor vehicles were not enough to ensure that the front lines were properly supported. By late 1944, when fuel was at a premium, it was the Panzers, halftracks and other equally important fighting vehicles that were given priority for the dwindling supplies of fuel. Consequently many of the support vehicles ran out of fuel and fell easy prey to the enemy.

LEFT: During the drive from Northern Finland to Murmansk, an adapted halftrack personnel carrier travels along a road, carrying a group of *Gebirgsjäger* officers from the 3rd *Gebirgs-*Division. The division remained in this sector until the autumn of 1942, when it was finally moved to the southern sector of the front. In late 1942, the division took part in the attempt to relieve the Sixth Army at Stalingrad. All the officers are wearing the mountain cap or *Bergmütze*. The *Bergmütze* was worn by all ranks of mountain units, ski units and *Jäger* personnel.

RIGHT: Summer 1941, and during his momentous drive as part of Army Group Centre, General Heinz Guderian and his staff confer over a map. To Guderian's left is his Horch light staff car. The vehicle, with license WH 656652, is fitted with an early pattern of the general's vehicle pennant on the right mudguard and a *Panzergruppe* commander's command flag on the left mudguard. In the background, a column of armoured vehicles can be seen. In the blistering heat, the crew sitting on top of the Pz.Kpfw.III have removed their shirts, wearing only the black Panzer *Feldmütze*.

BELOW: July 1943, and during Operation Citadel a crewmember of a Horch cross-country car is crudely applying a coat of paint to his vehicle. By this period of the war, a Panzer division had 130–180 tanks organized into a two- or three-battalion tank regiment, a Panzergrenadier brigade and an artillery regiment, and had about 250 or more vehicles in the support units. But, formidable as it seemed, it was still not enough. Even the support units were suffering from huge shortages of vehicles. As a consequence, many captured vehicles were used to support the attack through the Kursk salient.

ABOVE: Summer 1942, the Caucasus – a Horch Kfz.15 cross-country car from the 1st *Gebirgs*-Division tows a Pak 35/36 antitank gun. Supplying forces in mountainous regions in southern Russia was particularly difficult, especially when the support units were constantly being hampered by the terrain, narrow roads, and increasing partisan activity. This particular Horch vehicle is crossing a prefabricated bridge. Behind it, an Opel *Blitz* truck can be seen, laden with troops.

ABOVE: A support vehicle comes to the aid of a stricken tank that needs mechanical assistance on the battlefield. The support vehicles crane was necessary to lift or remove heavy parts for repair. Repairing a tank on the battlefield was the quickest way for vehicles to be returned to combat, as it was time consuming for them to be transferred to specialized workshops. During an armoured advance through the desert there were a number of independent battalions that were well equipped with maintenance companies. Much of the *Panzerwaffe* owed their success to them.

RIGHT: Troops from an unidentified *Gebirgs* regiment in southern Russia in 1942 try to relieve a support vehicle that has slipped down a ditch. The car has drawn the attention of local villagers and a number can be seen watching the spectacle. Moving an armoured division by road was an immense undertaking, especially when considering that a normal armoured column occupied nearly 112km (70 miles) of road space at any one time. Because wheeled vehicles did not have priority on the roads, they were frequently forced to one side to allow armour to push through.

ABOVE: The crew of a medium Horch cross-country car have underestimated the depth of this fast-flowing river and paid the price. In all likelihood the water has caused the engine to stall and any prospect of re-starting is impossible unless the car can be moved to dryer ground. To make matters worse, the vehicle is heavily laden with supplies, increasing the crew's burden. The tactical symbol painted on the rear of the vehicle indicates that it belongs to a signals unit.

BELOW: Members of the 4th SS Division *Polizei* on board a prime mover, which is towing a cart laden with supplies, in Russia in 1943. Wheeled transport was either pushed off the roads or towed through the worst stretches by tracked vehicles. Main roads were restricted to give priority to vehicles carrying fuel and ammunition. Food and other provisions were regarded as secondary. These supplies were carried by wheeled transport, which frequently became stuck or simply broke down, leaving exhausted troops at the front hungry and without the basic necessities to sustain them on the battlefield.

LEFT: Summer 1942, southern Russia – a Horch Kfz.15 queues on a riverbank. It has obviously been ferried across the river by engineers and is waiting to begin its journey with other support vehicles. This small river would not have presented a major obstacle to the Germans. That said, men and vehicles being ferried across any stretch of water was always a dangerous undertaking, especially if they came under attack. Enemy shells might not score a direct hit, but the waves from the explosion were sometimes enough to upset an overcrowded or overweight ferry.

ABOVE: Late summer 1943, southern Russia – a column of Horch cross-country cars travel along a road in a westerly direction. As the autumn of 1943 approached, and the prospect of another Russian winter, gloom and despair were slowly creeping in on the men of the German Army. The troops were on the retreat but were still deep inside the bleak and hostile landscape of the Soviet Union, always outnumbered and perpetually short of supplies of fuel and ammunition.

ABOVE: Supporting the 1st Panzer Army as it drives into the Caucasus, troops wait patiently for a long column of support vehicles to move off again. Meanwhile, a soldier from the 1st *Gebirgs*-Division reads one of the many signs and notices that has been attached to a tree. The condition of the narrow road means that it would only take one vehicle to develop a mechanical failure and break down, thereby halting the rest of the column.

RIGHT: Winter 1943, the Eastern Front – *Waffen-SS* troops from the *Das Reich* Division frantically attempt to relieve an armoured vehicle that has become stuck in the mud. It was often said that of while the cold killed the soldiers quickly in the East, it was the mud that broke the men's minds and spirits. Even the elite forces of the SS were not exempt from the hardships of mud: whole armies often slowed to a snail's pace and in some areas came to a standstill.

ABOVE: April 1941, the Balkans – a column of various support vehicles halts near a river, probably before continuing its advance southwards towards the Greek frontier. Hitler's *Blitzkrieg* in the Balkans secured another easy victory, but delayed the invasion of Russia by at least three weeks. Note the driver of one of the vehicles, who is wearing aviator goggles on his head. All the men are wearing the standard pattern army field-grey greatcoat and the M1938 *Feldmütze*.

BELOW: An unidentified artillery regiment in Poland in 1939, with support vehicles. The truck on the left has an artillery piece on the back. Carrying artillery was very unusual; the crews that had to manhandle them on board found the process time-consuming. The guns were either winched on board the vehicles by crane, or by ramp. Either way, transportation in this way was unconventional, and by 1940 virtually all artillery was towed by prime mover or horse.

ABOVE: During the Balkans campaign in April 1941, a long column of horse-drawn transport and a few trucks advance down a hillside road during the opening phases of the invasion. With the severe lack of transport motor vehicles, the German Army had to make extensive use of horse-drawn units, despite previous experience having shown that that horse-drawn transport could not keep up with motorized and tank units.

BELOW: Russia, and a variety of vehicles, including prime movers and Horch cross-country vehicles, travel along a dirt track. Both cars and trucks had to cover hundreds of miles, to keep up with the mechanized forces spearheading the advance. Gradually the supply lines became overstretched and vehicles that ran out of fuel or developed mechanical problems were often left tranded for hours, or even days.

LEFT: One of the many bridges destroyed during the Polish campaign in September 1939. Here, a bridge-building unit has erected a new bridge to allow advanced elements of the *Panzerwaffe* to continue their rapid advance east. A Pz.Kpfw.I moves along the road, and in the distance a Horch truck crosses the bridge. German ground forces, together with massive aerial support, were able to move with lightning speed and to great effect early in the war to achieve their objectives against a dazed and demoralized Polish Army.

ABOVE: During the invasion of the Low Countries, engineers erect a pontoon bridge across the Meuse river. German pioneer units were well practised in constructing pontoon bridges as rapidly as possible. It was imperative that the engineering trucks towing pontoon trailers and other bridging equipment kept pace with the advanced elements of the armoured spearhead. This particular pontoon bridge was one of the first constructed across the Meuse by Rommel's 7th Panzer Division. By the morning of 14 May 1940, the first of the pontoon bridges had been erected.

LEFT: On 20 May 1940, support vehicles cross a newly erected bridge over the Meuse river. Considerable damage can be seen on the buildings along the river banks. So swift was the drive towards the Meuse that it took a number of hours for the engineers with their support vehicles to arrive along the banks of the river. The successful crossing of the Meuse enabled the Panzer divisions of Army Group A to drive with all its fury northwards to the Channel coast and wreak havoc on the remnants of the British and French forces.

ABOVE: Horch vehicles are about to cross a 14.5-tonne (16-ton) pontoon bridge that has been erected across a river in southern Russia in 1942. The bridge-building units supporting the armoured spearhead closely in order to maintain the momentum of the advance were equipped with pontoons, barges and various rafts that were suitable for bridging most rivers or canals. Also carried were bridging platforms, which could take loads of 4.5–16 tonnes (5–17.6 tons).

ABOVE: Advancing through a French town ravaged by fire is a column of Opel *Blitz* trucks and Horch cross-country cars and a lone motorcyclist. These vehicles belong to the 25th Panzer Regiment of 7th Panzer Division, which was commanded by General Rommel. His division had advanced at speed through the wooded terrain of the Ardennes, and by 16 May 1940 the armoured units had moved across into France heading northwards through woods and villages. Ironically the fair condition of French roads such as this were of great benefit and contributed to the swiftness of German armoured advance.

LEFT: Russia, and an Opel *Blitz* truck hurtles through a flooded street. A typical Panzer division in 1941 comprised almost 3000 motor vehicles, including the supply column, and almost as many men as an infantry division (14,000 compared to 17,000). Nearly three-quarters of these men required transportation, and it fell to the many hundreds of support vehicles to provide this. Organizing transport fell to divisional headquarters, who were also responsible for organizing maintenance, rations, ammunition, supply, medical care, hygiene and sanitation.

ABOVE: This horse is probably being re-shoed, as indicated by the sign on the left. By 1942, the German Army on the Eastern Front was dependent on nearly 1,000,000 horses. However some 1000 horses died each day on average during the war with Russia. Consequently, a vast amount of organization was required for the rapid replacement of these animals, and this fell to the already overstretched support services. From all over German-occupied Europe and the occupied regions of the Soviet Union, long columns of vehicles brought in new horses to supplement the dwindling ranks.

LEFT: Two soldiers in Russia in 1942, fast asleep, are wearing the medical personnel badge – a yellow serpent and staff on a dark blue-green circular background. In order to distinguish those German troops who performed a specific military function and who had achieved proficiency in a specialist trade, special badges were introduced. Although some medical personnel were compelled to use horse-drawn transport, as in this photograph, the ambulance 25H Kfz.31 motor vehicle was a common sight among the support services.

ABOVE: Southern Russia, and soldiers from an unidentified *Gebirgsjäger* regiment are having extreme difficulties moving supplies along a dirt track. A number of soldiers have been busily digging the road, trying to make the surface as even as possible. The crew of an Sd.Kfz.7 watch their comrades struggling with the supply wagon. Moving across terrain like this was time-consuming and it only took a short downpour of rain to turn a dirt road into a quagmire.

ABOVE: July 1943, and prior to Operation Citadel these soldiers have set up temporary camp, having hidden their Opel *Blitz* truck and Sd.Kfz.251 halftrack beneath some trees. Both vehicles appear to be heavily laden with supplies. Canvas sheeting has been erected over the fighting compartment of the halftrack, probably to protect the troops from rain or the cold temperatures at night.

BELOW: The terrain on the Eastern Front was often hazardous to heavily-laden supply vehicles. Here an overweight Opel *Blitz* truck has careered down the side of a hill and smashed into another vehicle, and boxes of supplies litter the ground. Two crewmembers of an Sd.Kfz.7 halftrack survey the damage. One of the men is peering into the cab of the vehicle, presumably to see if there are any fatalities.

LEFT: The morning of 22 June 1941, and just hours after the initial attack across the Russian frontier support vehicles line up to begin the arduous task of supplying the forward advance of *Panzergruppe II*. This road is just west of the Bug river, where both bridges to the south of Brest-Litovsk fell, intact and undefended, at the first armoured rush. A Henschel and several Opel Blitz trucks tow pontoon trailers. Pontoon bridges were a vital asset to a Panzer division and a well-trained bridge engineering unit could construct a bridge in a matter of hours.

ABOVE: An Opel *Blitz* kitchen truck has been loaded on board a train for transportation to the Normandy sector in June 1944. By this period of the war, the quickest method of moving vehicles from one battlefront to another was by locomotive. However, this procedure was very dangerous, being vulnerable to aerial attack, and was normally undertaken only during the cover of night. Most of the troops are wearing the new form of military headdress, the *Einheitsfeldmütze*. This was introduced in June 1943 and became the most common form of headdress throughout the German armed forces.

LEFT: Summer 1942, southern Russia – Opel *Blitz* trucks, light Horch cars and a prime mover towing an sFH 18 heavy field howitzer move along a dusty road. These vehicles are attached to the XLIX Corps of Army B, which was one of the two new armies divided from the former Army Group South. The XLIX Corps was directed southwards to gain the Soviet oilfields of Baku, but barring access to the distant objective were the Caucasian mountains. This unit had been given the task of gaining the mountain passes before the onset of winter.

ABOVE: A soldier in Italy, 1943, poses for the camera next to his halftrack. A halftrack vehicle caused far less damage to the road surface than a tank and was only slightly less efficient than a fully tracked vehicle when moving across country. The halftracks not only towed artillery or were modified to carry flak guns, but also transformed the fighting quality of the armoured divisions. The versatility of the halftrack, though, created its own problems, for it was in constant demand, required to carry ammunition, lay cables, and evacuate casualties. It was also used for artillery observation.

ABOVE: During the opening phases of the invasion of Russia, various vehicles and motorcycle combinations from *Panzergruppe II,* commanded by General Heinz Guderian, have entered a town. These vehicles are probably part of Guderian's support services, because the town, which has seen some heavy fighting, had earlier been captured by forward echelons of the *Panzergruppe.* Within hours of the first lightning strike, Guderian's units had secured the area. Such rapid armoured penetration however had the commanders worried that they were overstretching the supply lines.

ABOVE: Early winter 1942, and an Sd.Kfz.6 halts on a muddy road to tow a staff car that has become bogged down in the mire. The halftrack vehicle has no markings visible through the layer of dried mud. In the foreground is a Soviet 45mm (1.77in) Model 1932 L/60 antitank gun that has been abandoned by the retreating Russian Army. This Russian gun weighed 510kg (1124lbs) in action and fired a 1.43kg (3.15lb) shell that was more than capable of penetrating 38mm (1.5in) of armour at an angle of 30 degrees at a range of 1000m (3282ft). It was used by the Red Army throughout the war.

RIGHT: A halftrack towing a Flak 88 gun and carrying armoured personnel passes a well dug in flak position in Russia, 1942. The halftrack performed a variety missions and became an integral element of the *Wehrmacht* armoury. They often supported the armoured drive, carrying troops and towing artillery, ammunition and other important supplies. They also worked in co-operation with both *Wehrmacht* and *Waffen-SS* tanks, artillery and self-propelled guns during battle.

BELOW: June 1944, Normandy – a German unit retreats. This town has probably been devastated by heavy Allied aerial bombing just prior to Operation Overlord. A host of vehicles stream through the smouldering ruins, trying in vain to reach a more secure position. In total, the Germans committed to the battle of Normandy some 400,000 men, leaving a further 250,000 in the Fifteenth Army expecting an invasion in the Pas de Calais. Within one month of the battle, Army Group B had sustained some 80,783 casualties and lost literally hundreds of tanks, self-propelled guns and support vehicles.

ABOVE: On the retreat through Russia a column of horse drawn transport and infantry move past various destroyed weapons and a dead horse. By this period of the war all the reserves were gone, the *Panzerwaffe* was now only a shadow of its former self. What was left of the armour was now loosely organized in ad hoc groups, often piecemeal. As logistical problems increased, many tanks and assault guns were rendered useless with insufficient fuel. Consequently, in a number of sectors the *Panzerwaffe* were compelled to abandon their tracked or wheeled vehicles and move either on foot or by horse transport. The last year of the war had become desperate days for the *Panzerwaffe*.

RIGHT: Moving steadily west, back towards the homeland an Sd.Kfz.7 towing a PaK gun follows horse drawn transport along a muddy road in Poland in late 1944. During the last days of 1944, with exception of a few intact Panzer units there were little mobile forces left to delay the Soviet onslaught. For many miles the *Panzerwaffe*, mingled with thousands of retreating civilians, strung out across a scarred and devastated wasteland as they retreated westward. The end was near.

GERMAN ARMOURED FORMATIONS BETWEEN 1939 AND 1945
PANZER INVENTORIES 1935–39

The inventory of tanks below shows the growth of tank numbers held by the *Panzerwaffe*, from division to division, starting from 1935 until just prior to the invasion of Poland in 1939.

TANKS

	Pz.Kpfw.I	Pz.Kpfw.II	Pz.Kpfw.III	Pz.Kpfw.IV	Pz.Kpfw.35(t)	Pz.Kpfw.38(t)	Command Light	Command Heavy
1 Aug. 1935	318							
1 Jan. 1936	720							
1 June 1936	1065							
1 Oct. 1936	1212	5					40	
1 May 1937	1411	115					72	
1 Oct. 1937	1468	238	12				163	
1 Jan. 1938	1469	314	23	3			180	
1 Apr. 1938	1468	443	43	30			180	
1 July 1938	1468	626	56	46			180	
1 Oct. 1938	1468	823	59	76			180	2
1 Mar. 1939	1446	1094	60	137			180	30
1 Sept. 1939	1445	1223	98	211	202	78	180	35
1 September 1939 with field army	1026	1151	87	197	164	57	177 total command tanks	
with reserves	260	67	11	11	34	5	20 total command tanks	

GERMAN PANZER FORCES

Wehrmacht
1st through 27th Panzer Divisions
116th Panzer Division
178th (Reserve) Panzer Division
179th (Reserve) Panzer Division
223rd (Reserve) Panzer Division
233rd Panzer Division
273rd (Reserve) Panzer Division
Clausewitz Panzer Division
1st *Felderrnhalle* Panzer Division
2nd *Feldherrnhalle* Panzer Division
Grossdeutschland Panzer Ersatz Brigade
Holstein Panzer Division
Jüterbog Panzer Division
Müncheberge Panzer Division
Norwegen (Norway) Panzer Division
Schlesien (Silesian) Panzer Division
Tatra Panzer Division
Panzer Lehr Panzer Division
Hermann Göring Panzer Division
101-113th Panzer Brigades

Norwegen (Norway) Panzer Brigade
Oberschlisen Panzer Brigade
West Schnelle Panzer Brigade
West Panzerjägd Panzer Brigade
Herman Göring Parachute Panzer Recruit and Training Brigade
2nd Herman Göring Parachute Panzer Recruit and Training Brigade

Waffen-SS
1st SS Panzer Division *Leibstandarte SS Adolf Hitler*
2nd SS Panzer Division *Das Reich*
3rd SS Panzer Division *Totenkopf*
5th SS Panzer Division *Wiking*
9th SS Panzer Division *Hohenstaufen*
10th SS Panzer Division *Frundsberg*
12th SS Panzer Division *Hitlerjugend*
26th SS Panzer Division
27th SS Panzer Division
28th SS Panzer Division
SS Panzer Brigade Gross

ORGANIZATION OF THE PANZER UNITS

1938

The internal organization of the Panzer regiment underwent constant change as the war progressed. Shown below is the organization of a Panzer regiment from 1 October 1938.

Regimental Staff
  Panzer Commander Troop
    (2 PzBefWg and 1 Pz.Kpfw.III tank)
  Panzer Signals Plantoon
    (5 Pz.Kpfw.II tanks)
2 Battalions, each with:
    Panzer Battalion Staff Company
      Panzer Signals Platoon
      (2 PzBeWg and 1 Pz.Kpfw.III tank)
      Panzer Signals Platoon (5 Mk II tanks)
        Commander Squadron (1 Pz.Kpfw.IV, 3 Pz.Kpfw.III
          and 2 Pz.Kpfw.II tanks)

3 Light Panzer Companies, each with:
      Command Troop (2 Pz.Kpfw.III tanks)
      Light Platoon (5 Pz.Kpfw.II tanks)
      1st–3rd Platoons (5 Pz.Kpfw.III tanks each)
The medium panzer companies were to contain:
  Command Troop (2 Pz.Kpfw.III tanks)
  Light Platoon (5 Pz.Kpfw.II tanks)
  1st–3rd Platoons (5 Pz.Kpfw.IV tanks each)
In addition an 'ersatz' company was organized as follows:
  1st Platoon (1 Pz.Kpfw.I, 1 PzBefWg and 5 Pz.Kpfw.I tanks)
  2nd Platoon (3 Pz.Kpfw.II tanks)
  3rd Platoon (3 Pz.Kpfw.III tanks)
  4th Platoon (3 Pz.Kpfw.IV tanks)

1939

Below is a typical organization of a panzer division at the beginning of the war in 1939. This organization was maintained until just after the invasion of France.

1 Panzer Brigade
  2 Panzer Regiments, each with:
    2 Panzer Battalions, each with:
      2 Light Panzer Companies
    1 Mixed Panzer Company
    Light Armoured Column
  1 Armoured Repair Shop Company
***Schützen* Brigade**
(4th and 5th Pz had no schützen brigade staff)
  1 (mot) *Schützen* Regiment, with
    2 Battalions, each with:
      2 *Schützen* Companies (Infantry companies)
        (9 LMGs, 2 HMGs, 3 50mm (1.97in) Mortars each)
      1 Motorcycle Company, with
        (9 LMGs, 2 HMGs, 3 50mm (1.97in) Mortars)
      1 Machine Gun Company
        (8 HMGs, 6 80mm (3.15in) Mortars)
      1 (mot) Infantry Column
1 Motorcycle Battalion, with
  3 Motorcycle Companies (9 LMGs, 2 HMGs, 3 50mm
    (1.97in) Mortars each)
  1 Motorcycle Machine Gun Company (8 HMGs and 6
    80mm (3.15in) Mortars)
  1 Heavy Company
    1 (mot) Anti-Tank Platoon (3 37mm (1.47in) PAK 36)
    1 (mot) Infantry Gun Platoon (2 75mm (2.95in) IeIG)
    1 (mot) Pioneer Platoon
1 (mot) Reconnaissance Battalion, with
  2 Armoured Car Squadrons
  1 Motorcycle Squadron (9 LMGs, 2 HMGs and 3 50mm
    (1.97in) Mortars)
  1 Heavy Motorcycle Squadron (8 HMGs and 6 80mm
    (3.15in) Mortars)
  1 (mot) Supply Column
1 Anti-Tank Battalion
(4th and 5th Pz Div had 2 *Panzerjäger* Bns)
  3 (mot) Anti-Tank Companies (12 37mm (1.47in) PAK 36)

1 (mot) Heavy Machine Gun Company
  (not in 2nd and 5th Pz Divs) (12 20mm (0.79in)
  Flak guns)
1 (mot) Artillery Regiment
  1 (mot) Heavy Artillery Battalion, with
    2 (mot) Batteries (4 150mm (5.9in) sFH each)
    1 (mot) Battery (4 100mm (3.94in) guns)
  1 (mot) Light Artillery Battalion, with 3 (mot) Batteries
    (4 105mm (4.13in) leFH 18 each)
  (In 2nd Pz Div 1 light and 1 heavy Artillery Bn, Heavy
    having 150 mm (5.9in) howitzers)
1 (mot) Pioneer Battalion, with
  3 (mot) Light Pioneer Companies (9 LMGs each)
  1 (mot) Bridge Column K or B
  1 (mot) Light Pioneer Column
    (4th Pz had 1 Pioneer Co, 1 Bridge Column, 1 (mot)
      Pioneer Column – 5th Pz like 4th Pz, but with 2
      Pioneer cos.)
1 (mot) Signals Battalion, with
  1 (mot) Radio Company
  1 (mot) Signals Company
  1 Light Signals Column
Medical Services
  2 (mot) Medical Companies
  3 Ambulance Platoons
Supply Services
  6 Light Small Motor Transport Columns
  3 Large Motor Transport Columns for Fuel
  2 (mot) Repair Shops
  1 (mot) Supply Company
Administrative Services
  1 (mot) Bakery Company
  1 (mot) Butcher Platoon
  1 (mot) Rations Officer
Other
  1 (mot) Military Police Detachment
  1 (mot) Field Post Office

1941

The organization of a panzer division in 1941 was as follows:

1st Panzer Division
  1st Panzer Regiment
    1 Armoured Signals Platoon
    1 Light Armoured Platoon
    1 Regimental Band
    1 (mot) tank Maintenance Company
  2 Armoured Battalions, each with
    1 Staff Company (2 PzBefWg III and 5 Pz.Kpfw.II)
    1 Medium Armoured Company (14 Pz.Kpfw.IV and 5 Pz.Kpfw.II)
    2 Light Armoured Companies (17 Pz.Kpfw.III and 5 Pz.Kpfw.II each)

1 Tank Maintenance Company
1 Light (mot) Armoured Supply Column
1st *Schützen* Brigade
  1st and 113th *Schützen* Regiments, each with:
  1 (mot) Staff Company, with
    1 (mot) Signals Platoon
    1 (mot) Engineer Platoon (3 LMGs)
    1 Motorcycle Platoon
    1 Regimental Band
  2 (mot) Battalions, each with
    3 Infantry Companies (18 LMGs, 2 HMGs, 3 50mm (1.97in) mortars each)

1944

The organization of a panzer division in 1944 was as follows:

Regimental Staff and Staff Company
  Staff
  Staff Company
    3 Panther MK V tanks (Sd.Kfz.171) with 75mm (2.95in) 42 L/70 guns
  Reconnaissance Platoon
    5 Panzer Mk IV, Sd.Kfz.161/2, 75mm (2.95in) 40 (L/48) guns
Battalion and Staff and Staff Company (Panzer IV Battalion)
  Staff
  Staff Company
    3 Panzer IV (75mm (2.95in) 40 (L/48) (Sd.Kfz.161/2)
    2 Sd Kfz 251/8
  Reconnaissance Platoon
    5 Panzer IV (75mm (2.95in) 40 (L/48) (Sd.Kfz.161/2)
  Reconnaissance and Pioneer Platoon
    3 Sd Kfz 3 or 3-ton (2.95t) truck
    3 Sd.Kfz.251/7 half-track
  Anti-Aircraft Platoon
    3 quad 20mm (0.79in) Flak guns
    3 Sd.Kfz.7/1 half-tracks
Battalion Staff and Staff Company (Panther Battalion)
  Staff

Staff Company
  3 Mk V Panther tank Sd.Kfz.171 – 75mm (2.95in) KwK 41 (L/70)
  2 Sd.Kfz.251/8
Reconnaissance Platoon
  5 Mk V Panther tank Sd.Kfz.171 – 75mm (2.95in) KwK 41 (L/760)
Reconnaissance and Pioneer Platoon
  3 Sd.Kfz.3 or 3-ton (2.95t) truck
  3 Sd.Kfz.251/7 half-track
Anti-Aircraft Platoon
  3 quad 20mm (0.79in) Flak guns
  3 Sd.Kfz.7/1 half-tracks
Medium Panzer Company (17 tanks)
  Staff
    2 Panther tanks, Sd.Kfz.171, 75mm (2.95in) 42 (L/70)
    or 2 Pz.Kpfw.IV, Sd.Kfz.161/2, 75mm (2.95in) 40 (L/48)
    or 2 Pz.IV/70A 75mm (2.95in) 42 (L 70)
  1st–4th Platoons
    5 Panther tanks, Sd.Kfz.171, 75mm (2.95in) 42 (L/70)
    or 5 Pz.Kpfw.IV, Sd.Kfz.161/2, 75mm (2.95in) 40 (L/48)
    or 5 Pz.IV/70A 75mm (2.95in) 42 (L 70)

1945

In March 1945, the last reorganization of the panzer divisions occured with the creation of the Type 45 Panzer Division organization. This final formation reorganized the remaining forces of the *Panzerwaffe*. The organization of a Type 45 Panzer Division was as follows:

Division Headquarters (420 men total)
  1 Division Staff (2 LMGs)
  1 (mot) Divisional Mapping Section
  1 (mot) Military Police Troop (5 LMGs)
  1 (mot) Division Escort Company
    1 Motorcycle Messenger Platoon (6 LMGs)
    1 (mot) Panzergrenadier Platoon (2 HMGs, 6 LMGs and 2 80mm (3.15in) mortars)
    1 Self-Propelled Flak Platoon (4 20mm (0.79in) Flak guns)

Mixed Panzer Regiment (1,361 men total)
  1 (Armoured) Panzer Regiment Staff (126 men: 6 LMGs and 2 75mm (2.95in) KwK)
  1 (mot) Panzer Regiment Staff Company
    1 Staff Platoon
    1 Staff Signals Platoon
1st (Panzer) Battalion (767 men total)
  Staff (1 LMG)
  Staff Company (12 LMGs)
    Staff Platoon

Armoured Pioneer Platoon
2 Panzer Companies (10 Pz.Kpfw. IV tanks each)
2 Panzer Companies (10 Pz.Kpfw. V tanks each)
1 Armoured Flak Company
    1 Panzer Flak Platoon (8 37mm (1.46in) Pz Flak 43
    and 8 LMGs)
    1 Self-Propelled Flak Platoon (3 quad 20mm (0.79in))
1 Panzer Maintenance Company (1 LMG)
1(mot) Panzer Supply Company (3 LMGs)

2nd (Panzergrenadier) Battalion (488 men total)
1 Armoured Staff (4 LMGs)
1 Armoured Staff Company (7 LMGs and 6 75mm
    (2.95in) PAK 40)
3 (armoured) Panzergrendier Companies (21 LMGs, 3
    Sd.Kfz.25/21 with triple 20mm (0.79in) guns and 1
    sturm platoon with *Sturmgewerb* 44 each)
1 Armoured Heavy Gun Platoon (7 75mm (2.95in) KwK
    and 1 LMG)
1 (mot) Supply Company (1 LMG and 3
    panzerschrecke)

2 (mot) Panzergrenadier Regiments, each with
1 (mot) Staff (48 men total; 3 *panzerschrecke*)
1 Staff Company (4 LMGs)
1 Signals Platoon
1 Motorcycle Messenger Platoon (4 LMGs)
1 (mot) Battle Column

2 (mot) Panzergrenadier Battalions (117 men total)
(mot) Staff (3 *panzerschrecke*)
    3 Panzergrenadier Companies (117 men per
    company; 12 LMGs, 3 *panzerschrecke* and 1 sturm
    platoon with *Sturmgewehr* 44 each)
    1 (mot) Machine Company (121 men; 8 HMGs, 6
    20mm (0.79in) Flak and 1 LMG)
    1 (mot) Heavy Company (127 men)
    Medium Mortar Platoon (8 80mm (3.15in) mortars
    and 6 LMGs)
    Heavy Mortar Platoon (4 120mm (4.72in) and 2
    LMGs)
1 (mot) Supply Company (77 men; 2 LMGs and 3
    panzerschrecke)
1 (motZ) Heavy Infantry Gun Company (102 men; 4
    150mm (5.9in) sIG)
1 (mot) Pioneer Company (144 men; 9 LMGs and 9
    panzerschrecke)

Panzer Reconnaissance Battalion (648 men)
1 (mot) Staff (1 LMG and 1 20mm (0.79in) KwK)
1 (armoured) Mixed Armoured Car Company (10
    75mm Kwk, 2 Sd.Kfz.251/21 with triple 20mm
    (0.79in), 8 20mm (0.79in) KwK, 18 LMGs)
2 Light (mot) Reconnaissance Companies (Volkswagen)
    (4 HMGs, 9 LMGs and 2 80mm (3.15in) mortars each)
1 (mot) Supply Company (1 LMG)

Mixed *Panzerjäger* Battalion (522 men)
Staff and Staff Company (2 Jagdpanzers and 1 LMG)
2 Jagdpanzer Companies, each with
    1 Panzergrenadier Escort Platoon (10 Jadgpanzer and
    10 LMGs)
    1 Self-Propelled *Panzerjäger* Company (9 75mm
    (2.95in) PAK and 1 LMG)
    1 (mot) Supply Company

Panzer Artillery Regiment (1,367 men)
    1 Panzer Artillery Regimental Staff and Staff Battery
    (2 LMGs)

1st (self-propelled) Armoured Battalion

1 (self-propelled) Battalion Staff and Battery (2 LMGs
    and 3 20mm (0.79in) mountain Flak guns)
2 Light Self-Propelled 105mm (4.13in) Batteries
    (6 105mm (4.13in) leFH Sd.Kfz.124 *Wespe* and 4
    LMGs)
1 Heavy Self-Propelled 150mm (5.9in) Battery (6
    150mm (5.9in) sFH Sd.Kfz.165 *Hummel* and 4
    LMGs)

2nd (mot) Battalion
1 (mot) Battalion Staff and Battery (2 LMGs and 3
    (motZ) 210mm (8.27in) mountain Flak guns)
2 (mot) Light 105mm (4.13in) leFH Batteries
    (105mm (4.13in) leFH 18 and 5 LMGs each)

3rd (mot) Battalion
1 (mot) Battalion Staff and Battery (1 Sd.Kfz.251, 3
    artillery observation vehicles with 3 LMGs and 3
    20mm (0.79in) mountain Flak Guns)
2 (motZ) Heavy 105mm (4.13in) Batteries (4 150mm
    (5.9in) sFH 18 and 4 LMGs each)
1 (motZ) 100mm (3.94in) Gun Battery (4 100mm
    (3.94in) K 18 and 4 LMGs)

Army Flak Battalion
1 (mot) Flak Battalion Staff and Staff Battery (2 LMGs)
2 (motZ) Heavy Flak Batteries (6 88mm (3.46in),
    3 20mm (0.79in) and 2 LMGs each)
1 (motZ) Light Flak Battery (9 37mm (1.46in) Flak 43
    and 3 self-propelled quad 20mm (0.79in) Flak guns)

Armoured Pioneer Battalion (716 men)
1 Pioneer Battalion Staff (9 LMGs)
1 (mot) Staff and Supply Company (4 LMGs)
1 Bridging Column
2 (mot) Pioneer Companies (2 HMGs, 18 LMGs, 2
    80mm (3.15in) mortars each)
1 (armoured) Pioneering Company (19 LMGs and 2
    HMGs)

Armoured Signals Battalion (378 men)
1 (mot) Armoured Signals Battalion Staff
1 Armoured Telephone Company (11 LMGs)
1 Armoured Radio Company (19 LMGs)
1 (MOT) Signals Supply Column (2 LMGs)

Feldersatz Battalion (173 men)
4 companies (50 LMGs, 12 HMGs, 6 80mm
    (3.15in) mortars, 2 120mm (4.72in) mortars, 1
    20mm (0.79in) Flak, 2 flamethrowers and 1
    105mm (4.13in) leFH)

Panzer Supply Group (702 men)
1 Panzer Supply Troop Regimental Staff and Staff
    Company (2 LMGs)
4 (mot) 120 ton (118t) Transportation Companies (4
    LMGs each)
3 (mot) 30 ton (29.5t) Transportation Squadrons (2
    LMGs each)
1 (mot) Weapons Maintenance Company (2 LMGs)

Vehicle Maintenance Troop (277 men)
2 (mot) Maintenance Companies (2 LMGs each)
1 (mot) 75 ton (73.8t) Maintenance Supply Column

Administrative Services (206 men)
1 (mot) Administrative Service Company (3 LMGs)
1 (mot) Bakery Platoon
1 (mot) Butcher Platoon
1 (mot) Administrative Platoon

Medical Troops (334 men)
1 (mot) Medical Company (2 LMGs)
1 Ambulance Company (1 LMG)

INDEX